Dirk Lauwaert. Selected Writings, 1983–2008

The Lieven Gevaert Series is a major series of substantial and innovative books on photography. Launched in 2004, the Series takes into account the ubiquitous presence of photography within modern culture and, in particular, the visual arts. At the forefront of contemporary thinking on photography, the books offer new insights on the position of the photographic medium within art historical, theoretical, social and institutional contexts. The Series is produced by the Lieven Gevaert Research Centre for Photography, Art and Visual Culture (www.lievengevaertcentre.be) and covers four types of approaches: publication of outstanding monographic studies, proceedings of international conferences, book length projects with artists, translations and republications of classic material. The Lieven Gevaert Series is published by Leuven University Press, and distributed in North America by Cornell University Press.

Series editors

Alexander Streitberger
Hilde Van Gelder

Lieven Gevaert Series vol. 33

Dirk Lauwaert
Selected Writings, 1983–2008

Edited by Herman Asselberghs, Robbrecht Desmet,
Bart Meuleman, Peter Jan Perquy

Translated by Sis Matthé and Trevor Perri

Leuven University Press

Table of Contents

Editorial Note

The occasion for publishing *Selected Writings* is the integration of the Dirk Lauwaert Collection in the Library of Sint-Lukas Brussels (LUCA School of Arts). Following the writer's death in 2013, his family loaned his enormous book collection to the school where he taught for many years, with the express wish that it be made accessible to researchers. Dirk Lauwaert's multilingual collection includes some eight thousand books on film, photography, fine art, architecture, urban planning, semiotics, philosophy, and more. Each book in the collection was carefully indexed by the librarians and added to the online library catalog. The collection is not only invaluable for its individual titles (many of the exhibition catalogs have become quite rare) but it also lends itself uniquely to interdisciplinary research due to its diverse nature. *Selected Writings* offers international researchers a first framework for working with the writer's collection.

This book has four editors, each with their own relationship to Lauwaert's work and memories of Dirk. Peter Jan Perquy is the head librarian at the Library of Sint-Lukas Brussels (LUCA School of Arts) and talked with Lauwaert about the donation and management of the collection. Since his death, these conversations have continued with his heirs. Robbrecht Desmet is a filmmaker, teacher, and researcher at LUCA. He never met or saw Lauwaert at work but got to know his writings while studying film. He now presents these writings to his own film students. Herman Asselberghs is a filmmaker and teacher at the same institute. In the 1980s, he discovered semiotics and experimental film through Lauwaert and started seeing Fred Astaire and Ginger Rogers in a different light. In the 1990s, as editor-in-chief of *Andere Sinema*, he invited Lauwaert to write on photography and many other subjects. At film school, they were fellow teachers. Bart Meuleman is a writer, poet, playwright, dramaturgist, and essayist. He is the literary executor of Lauwaert's work. They met in film school—Lauwaert a teacher, Meuleman a student—and became friends. During the author's lifetime, Meuleman edited three collections of texts with and for him, *Dromen van een expeditie*, *Lichtpapier*, and *De geknipte stof*. He recently edited Lauwaert's autobiographical texts in a new book titled *Zelfportret* (published by Bebuquin).

How to begin making a selection from thousands of texts? Texts of different lengths, originally published in various contexts, and written over the course of five decades. Their author can no longer have his say about his envisaged collection, his favorite typesetting, his desired page layout. He certainly would have held strong views about these things. His writings clearly point the way: the power of discourse takes precedence. Therefore, a book without images. With optimal readability—classic font, abundant white space, soft paper. A clear form to build on with an eye to introducing Lauwaert's complete Dutch-language oeuvre to readers from other language communities.

The consistent quality of Lauwaert's immense output is beyond dispute. The challenge is to present its depth and scope to new readers. One way would be to present Lauwaert as a chronicler, a critic pur sang, a reporter in the limelight. To do so would make for a collection of reviews, a weighty tome. Doing justice to his decades-long stream of film, book, and exhibition reviews would only be possible by putting this abundance on the table chronologically. For *Selected Writings*, the editors have opted for a different route: a constellation of various pieces in which Lauwaert fully displays his kaleidoscopic thinking and essayistic ability. In these key texts, the author discusses his central ideas and motifs, which are put into practice in chronicles and reviews elsewhere. His reflections (in the opening texts of this book) on the importance of experience and enthusiasm underpin his entire writing practice. His sketches of prominent members of his family of affinity (Serge Daney, Roland Barthes) and crucial roles (the intellectual, the critic, the amateur, the teacher) provide us with possible exemplary roles in the form of complicated self-portraits. Or is it the other way around? In any case, the statements of principle and role models generate thoughts about film, photography, and fashion that are invariably linked to questions of looking and showing. The sections deliberately lack titles, which would congeal Lauwaert's agile thinking. Preference was given to numbering, so that the grouping of texts could retain its porosity. For a text about moving images undoubtedly also talks about experience and passion and relates to teaching and refers to other images and to other thinkers and … The final text in the book concerns a farewell, in particular Lauwaert's decision to no longer write about contemporary art. Considering his ultimate break with film and his yo-yo relationship with photography, the "farewell" might as well be a "statement of principle" for him.

Selected Writings has few notes. With good reason: Lauwaert did not like them. No doubt he regarded notes in or at the bottom and even at the end of the text as obstacles to his train of thought. His essayistic pace could easily do without them. In this book, therefore, endnotes are presented at the back. This position does not make them less important: the first note to each text gives the date, place, and location of its original publication. Lauwaert's habit of mentioning names, titles, and terms without further explanation was, if necessary or desirable, met with short annotations (in the case of overly cryptic references or possible confusion as to the correct interpretation or historico-geographical publication context). No doubt the readers are in for the pleasure of their own research if the many threads of this weave are to be connected and reknotted.

Acknowledgements

For their generous support and thoughtful insights, the editors would like to thank

Hilde Van Gelder and the Lieven Gevaert Centre, Veerle Van der Sluys, Kristien Langenakens, Maarten Vanvolsem, Klaas Tindemans, Sis Matthé, Trevor Perri, Gerard-Jan Claes, Pepa De Maesschalck, Tillo Huygelen, Michel Kolenberg, Pim Dinghs, Steven Humblet, Reinhilde Weyns, Andreas & Dorian Lauwaert.

A Culture of Showing

Firm Elegance in the Writing of Dirk Lauwaert

Herman Asselberghs

The gaze starts from the back. There we see
how they watch: bent forward or backs straight,
arms supporting or behind them. Thus
the body modulates the gaze. A play between
judging from a distance and studying up close
(between synthesis and analysis, idea and detail).

Two women and three men. One arranges and
connects, but there is always one too many.
Destined to stay with the five of them. The
odd: binding balance.

One sits down to listen. That hand by her
left ear: "Am I right in hearing (what I see)?"

This is how Dirk Lauwaert writes about *Admiration* (1860), an albumen
print by the French-Spanish amateur pioneer of photography Olympe
Aguado. However compact the text that accompanies this modestly
sized image (20.4 cm by 15.2 cm), it unfolds a whole world of looking.
His words make one look at looking.[1]

Dirk Lauwaert (1944–2013): Belgian critic and essayist, writer, and teacher. Over the course of nearly five decades, he regularly published on film, photography, fashion, visual arts, and everything cultural. His pieces appeared in Flemish and Dutch cultural magazines such as *Film & Televisie*, *Kunst en Cultuur*, *Knack*, *Versus*, *Skrien*, *Andere Sinema*, *Obscuur* (all no longer active), *De Witte Raaf* (still alive and kicking), and in the culture supplement of the daily newspaper *De Financieel-Economische Tijd* (now *De Tijd*). He wrote for exhibition catalogs, made radio features, and contributed to television programs. For twenty-five years, he taught at the Brussels art schools Sint-Lukas (today LUCA School of Arts Brussels) and RITS (now RITCS School of Arts). His continuous production of texts and presence in the classroom inspired generations of readers and students. Many of them went on to take their place in the arts landscape. On the Dutch-language island, Lauwaert is a significant name for many publicists, artists, curators, lecturers, researchers, and other cultural workers of a certain age. Not counting exceptions, he is now virtually unknown to a younger generation.

Artikels, an initial selection from Lauwaert's fragmented output, was only published in 1996, thirty years after his debut. Four more collections followed during his lifetime: *Dromen van een expeditie* (2006), *Lichtpapier. Teksten over fotografie* (2007), and *Onrust* (2011). *De geknipte stof* (2013) would appear posthumously.[2] On the occasion of the first and fifth anniversary of his death, the art magazine *De Witte Raaf*, in which he published some of his most substantial pieces for nearly twenty years from the early 1990s, took the first steps in opening up Lauwaert's extensive literary legacy—literally thousands of texts. Since then, the online film magazine *Sabzian* has contributed to a steadily growing collection of translations that introduce Lauwaert to the French- and English-speaking worlds.[3] On the tenth anniversary of his death, this book brings together fourteen of his many "flying sheets" in an academic series.[4]

Dirk Lauwaert writes about images—moving or still, historical or contemporary, overfamiliar or unseen. He experienced them intensely, studied them attentively, and subsequently linked their forms with ethical, philosophical, or social issues in texts that invite their readers to do the same when leaving the movie theater, browsing a photography book, or visiting an exhibition. The cinematic experience impressed him early on. At first, there were school screenings of Chaplin as well as Laurel and Hardy at Jesuit College and the lasting impact of a young Romy Schneider in the popular Sissi trilogy.[5] Then, in the late 1950s, there was the local Catholic Cinéclub where he discovered film as an art form through the new European auteur cinema. In the early 1960s, a trip to Paris would leave an indelible impression, the capital forever remaining a pole of intellectual and cultural attraction. For a long time, in his teens and early twenties, he filled diary after diary with life questions and annotated lists of books he was reading, LPs he was listening to, and films he was watching. Until he firmly switched to being a public author: his fledgling contributions to the university magazine *Universitas* in 1965 set the stage for a lifelong career as a critic. From the very start, despite the permanent deadlines and imposed formats of writing for a living, he considered criticism to be more than consumer advice. Writing was his vocation, criticism a duty and, like teaching, they are a conduit of passionate knowledge and informed sensibilities, of an enthusiastic attitude.

No true reader of Lauwaert's wide-ranging work can ignore it: his massive intellectual legacy is spread across a handful of (substantial) text collections, a few separate publications, many forgotten periodicals, various catalogs and, since his death, online versions of some articles. One weighty tome just never came about. No commentator will fail to notice that both in his disordered oeuvre and in (almost) every single piece of text, systematics loses out to chronicling. A seasoned reviewer of films, books, and exhibitions, Lauwaert is a master of reporting. He proceeds from one piece to the next, in each case managing to squeeze his impressions and insights into the prescribed lengths and formats. Even his more comprehensive texts, in which he allows himself detours and shortcuts, bear evidence of a high output. The next sentence, the next paragraph, the next idea (like the next image in a film) rarely takes long. The writing, however, is never a rushed job or an incitement to cursory reading. With this writer, velocity is a sign of vitality.

The signature style of this prolific writer is recognizable out of thousands. Vintage Lauwaert looks as follows: precisely worded, crystal-clear insights alternate with unresolved, nebulous thoughts. The text is brazenly subjective, demonstrating an erudite frame of reference and theoretical baggage. Verbal arabesques, glissades, and pirouettes: thinking proceeds along an elegant choreography with no floorplan to speak of. The reader must try to keep up. Each paragraph group briefly brings the concentrated train of thought to a halt. As if the writer abandons a winding train of thought before he has completed it. Or even before the reader has completely grasped it. Again and again, one braces oneself for yet another démarche in his dancing considerations. After reading the final sentences, it's time to exhale vigorously.

In Lauwaert's pedagogical reflections, teaching becomes dosing, looking for the right measure. The teacher's task is to find the appropriate speech, an objective that also applies to the writer. He tries to subtly balance presence with the right words and the right silences. "With words, he tries to temper the deafening noise of the silent presence of an image. While speaking, he conjures it, welcomes it, gives it a place, so that it can become attached, leave traces."[6] Elsewhere, the author specifies his speaking, "Reflection that does not first neutralize the experiences only to never return to them but is as close as possible to those experiences. [...] This ultimately means not hardening the work into a document—but trying to grasp it in the moment and form of its appearance."[7] When it comes to teaching or writing, for Lauwaert, reflection can and must never coagulate. Momentary coagulation of thought is inevitable when it is cast in text, but even then mental agility remains an end rather than a means for this author, a way of countering closure and completion with all one's might. One of his collections of texts is called *Onrust* [Restlessness] for good reason, since movement also includes agitation.

To be moved by movement: there is no doubt that the intensity of the film experience provides the fertile soil for Lauwaert's small philosophies of writing and teaching. Watching a film means surrendering to the drift of image and sound, to "naked presence and duration." By definition, writing and teaching happen after the facts. The report always comes afterward (possibly on the basis of notes made in the meantime). Like no other, Lauwaert deeply penetrates the tension between experience and articulation. How to reconcile the two? He knows it's impossible. "Experience is fundamentally obstinate toward the word, toward commentary. Especially toward methodical, ordered commentary, which forces (must force) the discussed subject into the straitjacket of its point of departure. Experience explodes that language, lures thinking away from itself, on several paths at once, in a contradictory and paradoxical way. Hence another language strategy, that of criticism in the form of poetry: didactic poems. Not the expression of emotions or events, but the struggle to see and know, as close to experience as possible."[8] Articulation, in the classroom and on paper, leans against experience but does not ever coincide with it. The gap between experience and reflection is where teachers, critics, and essayists operate. Always in the moment but after the fact. Afterward, Lauwaert says, the words "only belong to the work like a bowl belongs with the fruit, a pedestal under a sculpture, a wooden frame around a photograph: as a means of stirring attention and expressing appreciation."[9]

This well-considered writing practice would find its breeding ground in a full and erratic trajectory that was invariably intertwined with professional worries. In the first half of the 1960s, Lauwaert's studies in communication sciences at the Catholic University of Leuven failed to hold his attention. He followed it up by attending the program in film directing at the Centro Sperimentale in Rome, which was de facto on strike as part of the student and worker protests. At the end of the sixties, those turbulent years of study made for an exquisite reading, watching, and talking laboratory, the city a school of the good (city) life. Once back in Belgium and having concluded that he would never become a filmmaker himself, he began the 1970s as the culture editor for the Catholic-tinged weekly *Spectator*, where he would write about film, television, literature, opera, sociology, and pedagogy. In 1970 he switched to the monthly magazine *Kunst & Cultuur* and later, too, to the liberal daily *De Nieuwe Gazet*, where he wrote about literature, history, visual arts, and photography.

Meanwhile, a doctoral track at the Center for Communication Sciences in Leuven would come up, in the form of a position as assistant. At the very end of the 1970s, the development of his dissertation brought him to the École pratique des hautes études (EPHE) in Paris, where he wanted to study semiotics with Roland Barthes but ended up with Algirdas Greimas and Jean-Paul Aron. As each other's opposites, they fed Lauwaert's lifelong intellectual passions: on the one hand, semiotics and the structuralist analysis of the work of art; on the other, the sociological-historical study of the conditions of existence for art and culture. He would never obtain his doctorate (titled *Het beeld van de intimiteit* [The image of intimacy], with *All That Heaven Allows* by filmmaker Douglas Sirk as its central object of study). Disappointed by the institute's negative reaction, he literally dumped the draft of his dissertation in the trash can. Once the assistantship ended, his departure from the university became definitive. At the start of the 1980s, his future seemed to remain in art schools, where he lectured to film and photography students.

Over the next three decades, Lauwaert's reputation as a writer and teacher grew. He published nonstop, regularly talked about films and exhibitions on Flemish radio. Until well into the 1990s, he contributed to notorious (and long forgotten) art magazines such as *Het gerucht*, *Verwant*, and *Ziggurat* on national television. He organized workshops and courses in art centers. He started writing about photography more seriously.[10] He gave lectures and introduced film screenings. For the Amsterdam Film Museum, he put together a film program with archival copies of early cinema. Together with the British artist Craigie Horsfield, he curated an exhibition and a book on collaborationism for the Brussels Palais des Beaux-Arts.[11] He taught at P.A.R.T.S., the leading school for contemporary dance. At the beginning of the new century, he began to write about fashion and dress. He established Efemera, an interdisciplinary research group that focused on two distinct projects. *Picturingfashion* dealt with the representation of fashion in film. *Citygraphy* studied modern urbanity by way of late nineteenth-century, early twentieth-century urban photography from Maastricht, Bruges, Brussels, Bologna, Rome, and Ghent.[12] This subject matter potentially held out the prospect of a new doctoral track, this time at the University of Edinburgh. The diagnosis of an incurable brain tumor put the brakes on the never-ending string of writings and projects. In the final stretch, he produced five penetrating autobiographical essays, the ultimate proof of his bona fide authorship.[13]

In his later reflections on cinema, Lauwaert makes a clear, qualitative distinction between passionate moviegoers and detached consumers. The difference between the two is a matter of (dis)belief. The one deems film "not only an instrument of distance but also a wondrous way of being with the world,"[14] "albeit in a roundabout way that is simultaneously a revelation: a revealing distance."[15] The other is the product of "an ideal critical education with regard to images" and approaches film images "in a suspicious, even hostile, and contemptuous way."[16] The difference between the two lies in the importance that Lauwaert, throughout his work, attributes to experience. As a teacher, he hazards a lofty definition of the central concept: "The most important thing falls outside the realm of learning and teaching, namely, experience: that which addresses you exclusively and profoundly changes you. The appeal is unique, once only, unplannable: ultimately of the order of epiphany, of 'grace,' of the undeserved 'gift.'"[17] Those winged words count as an article of faith. In fact—surprisingly enough in an article on pedagogy—they subordinate pedagogy to revelation. The experience of the classroom is very similar to the situation of the movie theater that Lauwaert elsewhere refers to as "essential, sublime distance."[18] Between the lines, teaching and watching a film turn out to operate using the same curious formula: proximity through distance.[19]

Experience is the magic word in the Lauwaert lexicon. It is always about making the student and the reader "look into the eyes of the work" with a view to "creating the possibility of a 'first look' that unleashes infatuation."[20] Always on the lookout for the intensity of that original encounter. Hence, no doubt, his many beautiful and heartfelt paragraphs and whole pages in his writings devoted to his own childhood, to silent film, to nineteenth-century sensibilities in the arts (in many respects the century that gave rise to the twentieth century, and of course the origin of cinema). Hence also his growing cultural pessimism, his rising (intelligent) lamentation over just about anything of topical interest at the end of the last and the beginning of this century— contemporary art, the academization of higher education in the arts, contemporary cinema, television, information, current affairs. From that point of view, or rather, in that state of mind, experience as such is bound to be subject to decay, individually fading into memory or collectively replaced by experiences, by kicks and events.

Reading Lauwaert today means taking cognizance of a message from a past that seems to be receding ever faster and further. The cultural-social context in which his reflections took shape no longer corresponds to that of today. Many freelance writers who must obediently bend to today's briefings and templates will be surprised at Lauwaert's elbow room. He, too, wrote pretty much to order. He, too, had to adhere to prescribed lengths. But within that professional framework, he could genuinely write whatever he wanted. Without guidelines in terms of content or approach, the formats were usually reviews or requests to approach a theme in his own way—without any rules regarding style, tone, or structure. He radically embraced that editorial freedom—without apologies. For both the writer and the reader, the pieces make for intense issues. The dialogue with predecessors, examplars, and kindred spirits seems to take precedence over the conversation with his readers. The author expects from his audience the same prior knowledge, the same erudition, the same passion that he possesses. Those who are not in that position should just try to keep up. The best example of this stubborn refusal to clarify is his standard omission of the first names of authors and artists to which he refers "argumentatively," often between brackets and without any explanation or footnote whatsoever. Titles of films, books, and artworks repeatedly receive the same treatment. They are not necessarily unknown or far-fetched. If anything, they are chosen carefully and with reason. Ready knowledge of their status, though, is required for understanding their place in the discourse.

Rather than unreasonable self-evidence, Lauwaert's habit of careless namedropping may well be part of a self-proclaimed method of resistance. In that context, his piece on Roland Barthes at times reads as an allusion to self-scrutiny by way of the difference between the two of them: "More than anybody else, Barthes distrusts the authority of cultural tradition. He does not draw authority from culture. He distrusts erudition. In doing so, he misses an important other figure: erudition as resistance, culture as a challenge, the complexity of the past as a task. Culture is a brilliant and indispensable means of arming oneself against fashion."[21] These can only be the words of a chronicler, of an experienced reporter who continues to discern a story in the constant, unlimited cultural offerings, constructing his narrative through accumulating memory, broad interest, and great curiosity. Elsewhere, in his reflection on the role of the intellectual, he points to the writerly technical consequence of his continued confidence in (and deep familiarity with) cultural tradition. Writing appears as "a way of acting while thinking: no exposition, no argumentation, no logical method, exasperatingly implicit self-evidences that are not up for discussion. What's more, in his writing the aleatory plays an important role—the aleatory that characterizes everyday life. In that impure space, insights are not put into practice, conclusions are overlooked, predictable consequences irrationally ignored. The intellectual thinks impulsively and thus often inconsistently, according to his temperament. In the face of new information and insights, habit offers beneficial and sometimes catastrophic resistance. [...] His logic is always playful, his argumentation always a caricature, his arguments often one-sided. Yet he is concerned with something else; he must do justice to the complexity of the subject, to the elusive capriciousness and complexity of his own reactions to it."[22]

Writing around or beyond insightful information and clear communication does not always make things easier for the reader, including the motivated reader. Inevitably, every text must be taken seriously. Peter Delpeut, author and filmmaker and friend of Lauwaert, aptly expresses how this trait can play out when he recalls his response to the question of whether a publisher might still be found for some of Lauwaert's texts in the Netherlands: "Dirk's texts are considered difficult in the Netherlands, in a word that is increasingly employed over here (with assault-like doggedness, I dare say): *inaccessible*. I never told him in those exact words, but I did try to explain to him several times that he was playing 'for high stakes' with his writing style, which obstinately lacks argumentative leads that could take an unprepared reader by the hand in a friendly manner. In my reply to an email from December 2012, I now read, 'You do something with language that fascinates me. That is to say, you dawdle, you use language to slowly let a blot expand, not to progress linearly or argumentatively. I read a sentence. And another sentence. But the space in between isn't naturally filled in. Sometimes I manage to find the bridge, but sometimes I don't. It resembles your way of speaking when you are teaching or lecturing. Even then, you crawl along. You try a sentence, and again, and again, and out of those three together, as a listener you have to get that one statement or thought. But if you don't pay attention, the sentences slip right through your fingers. Usually it's the author who holds a text together. With the texts you write, it is the reader who has to make the effort of holding them together. It takes a lot of inventiveness on the part of the reader. And it is a great reward when it succeeds.'"[23] Which implies that it does not always succeed, that it does not always have to succeed. Few editors-in-chief or general editors today can afford to publish such a challenging piece.

Lauwaert could write whatever he wanted. That is the privilege of the pioneer. He could afford to skip first names, to refer to "obscure" photographs or films and consider these references obvious.[24] For despite his place in the mainstream media, he addressed a select audience for whom cultural education and the canon, reading, and museum visits were a matter of course, but for whom exhibitions in Paris, film screenings at international festivals or the film museum, and books in French, German, or English were not immediately within reach. Flanders had a central position between the important Western European cities of culture, but there was no high-speed train connection yet. Dutch translations of Roland Barthes or Serge Daney were rare or nonexistent. There were precious few exhibition venues for photography in Europe at the time.[25] In the first decades of his writing life, VCRs, DVD players, and satellite TV did not yet exist. Online availability and access only existed in the last decade of his career and life. During all those years, Lauwaert pointed out, showed, and opened up things. Even more than his readers, it was perhaps his Flemish students who, in their classrooms in the capital, learned about figures, works, and ideas whose existence they had never suspected or had only dreamed of. Not that Lauwaert limited himself to discussing what remained out of sight and out of reach. Quite the contrary, he spoke with as much ease, knowledge, and passion about popular cinema and television programs as he did about auteur cinema and experimental film, fashion photography, photography as art practice, painters of the nineteenth century, and contemporary visual artists. No doubt he held an introductory position here in this country but, more importantly, he taught his Flemish readers and listeners to watch differently, more thoroughly, and more sensitively.

In retrospect, it becomes clear how Lauwaert's new start as a reviewer in the first half of the 1970s pretty much coincided with the advent of the neoliberal regime and the beginning of the end of the welfare state. It was no accident that he saw his editorial freedom gradually curtailed twenty years later, when the compelling commercial and competitive logic of neoliberalism penetrated into all sections of the written press, radio and television broadcasting, and education. He (and with him many other contemporaries) was gently pushed out of the mainstream media and increasingly into the margins of specialized outlets and the back alleys of educational institutions. This forced removal no doubt contributed to the sharp tone of his later critical pieces, if not vehement analyses of anything reeking of conventional institutions. Yet Lauwaert's growing lamentation over the contemporary does not spring solely from a changing world. *Self-chosen* moving house is a common thread throughout his trajectory. The farewell is his modus operandi, a way to find that "first glance" again, to be able to relive an intense experience and write as close to it as possible. Invariably, the moment comes when he gets tired of things that have been close to his heart for a long time. When he stops writing about film in 2001, he had already formulated that farewell to his great passion six years earlier in *Dreaming of an Expedition*, perhaps one of his most beautiful texts. His break with contemporary art in 2000 yields one of his most vitriolic pieces, the clear-titled *Moving House*. Whenever he writes about photography, it seems as if the separation is about to happen any time. Sometimes love just ceases to exist? No, not quite. At some point, *infatuation* irrevocably ceases to exist.[26] In his portrait of Barthes, Lauwaert points out the operational difference between love and infatuation, which also characterizes his own attitude: "Love obliges, infatuation does not. The former is a law, the latter is ruleless—or at least it promises rulelessness. Barthes's entire oeuvre is governed by an elegant mechanism of evasion. The work has many infatuations, few great loves. [...] Barthes holds infatuation against love. This attitude explains the brilliant elegance of his work; a decorative sophistication that makes his entire work, every sentence, every theory read like a spiraling arabesque."[27]

The promise of rulelessness guarantees, at least for a period of time, the farthest possible distance from all institutional frameworks, which stand in the way of the intensity of any original (viewing) experience. Infatuation enables the "descent into that unknowable other," as he aptly describes teaching in *Reports from a Classroom*. Yet infatuation does not last, especially if it turns out to be based on a misunderstanding. Sensing that misunderstanding early and expressing it late seems to govern Lauwaert's greatest passions—film, photography, teaching. Along these lines, his portrait of Serge Daney, *The Rhythm of Thinking*, seems to be a hardly concealed self-portrait. Its concluding paragraph goes as follows: "'To try to hope desperately,' Daney says about television. But his whole oeuvre, his most intimate style, the core of his 'modus operandi' as a thinker, writer, polemicist, and inspirer bears the stamp of despair, a despair without slowness and laziness, which excites and drives him at ever greater speed: productive despair, demanding despair. If everything is based on a misunderstanding, the freedom to justify is all the greater and the desire to do so all the more irrepressible. That which one cannot change, one must at least try to think."[28] And thinking involves writing:

authorship is the one domain that, for Lauwaert, is not based on mis-understanding. Writing is a struggle, indeed. A clash and a showdown, sure. And a quarrel. But never a mistake. That infatuation remains.

Reading Lauwaert today means negotiating with the otherness of his texts.[29] Their privileged perspective is that of a bourgeois culture (which he never speaks disparagingly of but openly appreciates as a histori-cal project). Its blind spots are clearer today than ever before because they are peculiar to the position of a white, Western European man of the postwar middle class. Indeed, Lauwaert's intellectual and cultural frame of reference includes few women. His attention to non-Western cultural production is virtually nonexistent. Those looking for polit-ical positions on controversial contemporary issues (past or present) will leave empty-handed. Around the turn of the century, the writer sensed paradigm shifts (such as the radical democratization of the arts and the oversupply of images), but one can only surmise how he would have experienced the profound cultural transformations of the past few years. And what his response would have been to digital cinema, so-cial media, online education, or identity thinking at a time of ecological emergency. Not particularly enthusiastic, perhaps: he was usually quick to dismiss anything that was new and difficult or did not fit into the patterns he had in mind—oedipal patterns, in particular. His percep-tion of cinema as a story of fathers and sons, and more specifically of father-orphans, offered little room for existing feminist film histories and practices. Who today could, when reflecting on the figure of the dandy (yet another self-analysis?), do anything with statements such as "for women, the mirror is already the gaze of the opposite sex," "women are the principle of nature par excellence," or "at the same time, women are fascinating because they are ambiguous and elusive, capricious and pure appearance"?[30]

The question is also: who could do anything with it at the time? An acute case of gender blindness? Certainly. Reducing his entire oeuvre to just that and then canceling it? Certainly not. Reading requires finding a relationship to the text, to any text. Consequently, reading Lauwaert requires finding a relationship to his style, to his world. That world is necessarily situated and singular, as he himself points out when he compares the intellectual and the critic. "The intellectual manifests himself with his opinion in a social field, the critic, on the other hand, primarily in the realm of private sensibility which cannot, in the final analysis, be contested or argued. The critic must be excitingly unpredictable. The critic speaks on his own behalf; so does the intellectual but among and against others. The critic starts from an inner impulse, the intellectual from an impulse outside himself. The critic does not answer the fundamental social question but is given the chance to play the game of unjustified judgment."[31] Unpredictable and irresponsible, it is a game of luxury for those who can afford it. For Lauwaert, it is certainly a self-conscious game, a role-playing game. Because it is not entirely clear (to himself, in the first place?) who he sides with, the intellectual or the critic, he immediately comes out with a third role, that of the amateur (and this role too either suits or does not suit him). "The amateur is an entirely different story. He does not think in terms of educating others but of generous curiosity. [...] For him, every experience is a basis for radical irresponsibility. [...] His disposition discredits him, while it used to be the very basis of expertise. The curiosity of the amateur is a source of caution and endless nuances—which today are misunderstood as a lack of clear insight, organization, and consistency. The amateur thinks—but without metathought, without a method, without epistemological obsession. His thinking derives its particularity precisely from the absence of an objectifiable method."[32]

Radically subjective. Radically unapologetic. Radically demanding. For better or worse, these traits of Lauwaert's skill, attitude, and sensitivity are the result of radical attention. He looks and looks and looks again. He phrases and rephrases. Perhaps the lasting value and true actuality of his entire oeuvre lies in this practice of creating utmost attention. He is rarely clearer than in his plea for the importance of showing (of being allowed, willing, and able to show) in a culture of exchange: "I do not wish to be complicit in the increasing distraction of my fellow humans." For "against the gesture of 'giving' in showing stands the attitude of 'receiving' in looking. Both positions are the basis of every creation narrative, of every social relationship, of every recognition. For me, the elegance with which this complexity is perceived and experienced is at the heart of the showing of images—of what turns the showing into a culture. Distraction, however charming, however sophisticated, is not culture."[33] Firm words to read and engage with today, both in and outside the Dutch-speaking world.

Notes

1. Dirk Lauwaert, "Een kwintet," in *Affect/Afstand* (Leuven: Klapstuk 87, 1987).

2. *Artikels* (Brussels: Yves Gevaert Uitgever, 1996), *Dromen van een expeditie. Geschriften over film, 1971–2001* (Nijmegen: Uitgeverij Vantilt, 2006), *Lichtpapier. Teksten over fotografie* (Antwerp: FotoMuseum Provincie Antwerpen, 2007), *Onrust* (Ghent: het balanseer, 2011), and *De geknipte stof. Schrijven over mode* (Tielt: Uitgeverij Lannoo, 2013).

3. *De Witte Raaf* devoted extensive pieces to Lauwaert's life and work, accompanied by previously unpublished texts, in issues 171, 191, 192, and 193. They can be consulted (in Dutch) at www.dewitteraaf.be/archief/.

   See sabzian.be/authors/dirk-lauwaert for the list of online pieces published in Dutch, French, and English.

4. *Vliegende vellen* (*Flying Sheets*) (1983) is the title of a collection of short stories by the Dutch writer Ethel Portnoy. Lauwaert uses this term in his reflections on the intellectual, referring to Portnoy's book in a note: "The intellectual is an occasional thinker and writer. His form is the brief, time-bound intervention. A book doesn't suit him—his book is at most a collection of 'flying sheets.'" See Dirk Lauwaert, "Portret van een rol: de intellectueel," *De Witte Raaf* 75 (September–October 1998): 7–9.

5. The young Romy Schneider performed the role of the nineteenth Empress Elisabeth of Austria-Hungary three times, in *Sissi* (1955), *Sissi—The Young Empress* (1956), and *Sissi— The Fateful Years of an Empress* (1957), each time directed by Ernst Marischka. Fifteen years later, she takes on the same role in Luchino Visconti's *Ludwig* (1973). In 2013, Lauwaert writes about her in "Kijk, zonder mouwen! Chanel, Visconti en Romy Schneider 'at work,'" in *De geknipte stof. Schrijven over mode* (Tielt: Lannoo Publishers, 2013), 187–211.

6. Dirk Lauwaert, "Berichten uit een klas," in *Artikels* (Brussels: Yves Gevaert Uitgever, 1996), 41.

7. Dirk Lauwaert, "Hedendaags sofisme en de arme ervaring," in *Artikels*, 208.

8. Lauwaert, "Hedendaags sofisme en de arme ervaring," 216–217.

9. Lauwaert, "Hedendaags sofisme en de arme ervaring," 209.

10. Steven Humblet places the start of Lauwaert's reflections on photography in 1977, underlining the importance of the following decade for his (characteristically) wide-ranging and in-depth exploratory approach: "A production of ten years, according to Lauwaert, is about the time it takes for a critic to familiarize himself with the complex matter of a new and as yet unexplored medium. The texts are about photobooks, exhibitions, events, debates, and photographic theory, in exceptional cases also about photographic technique. They cover the wide range of photographic practice (reporting, documentary, fashion, architecture, landscape, portrait), some personal fascinations recurring remarkably often—for all forms of film photography, for nineteenth-century architecture and urban photography, for French humanist photography and modern photography of the interwar period." Steven Humblet, "'…een catastrofe, een revolutie; een omwenteling.' Dirk Lauwaert over fotografie," *De Witte Raaf* 191 (January–February 2018): 15.

11. The collaboration years are not just any random matter; they are part of a family history: Lauwaert's father's collaborationist war past can be considered a driving force of his self-proclaimed writing mission. An avid, sensitive handling of culture as a response to his parents' fascism? Obsessive writing as overwriting a black page, as the settling of a debt by the next generation? In the extensive dialogue with Craigie Horsfield, included in the publication that accompanies the Kessels exhibition, Lauwaert gives a very personal account of the profound impact of transgenerational trauma transmission on his passionate cultural-intellectual development: "Cinema has been particularly important because it was a commercial medium, which allowed me to escape from my family and cultural background. I chose cinema against my family." Erik Eelbode and Catherine Robberechts, *Geheugenverlies. Verantwoordelijkheid en collaboratie. Willy Kessels, fotograaf* (Brussels: Vereniging voor Tentoonstellingen van het Paleis voor Schone Kunsten, 1997), 141.

12. *Citygraphy* resulted in three eponymous publications, *Citygraphy #1* (Brussels: Efemera, 2007), *Citygraphy #2* (Brussels: Efemera, 2009), and *Citygraphy #3* (Brussels: Efemera, 2013), as well as three essays, "Stadsfotografie in het negentiende-eeuwse Brugge. Deel I: Tussen toerisme en restauratie," in *De Witte Raaf* 104 (July–August 2003): 15–20; "Stadsfotografie in het negentiende-eeuwse Brugge. Deel II: De mentaliteit van de beelden," in *De Witte Raaf* 105 (September–October 2003): 19–24; "'Tot aan de poort…': Over de iconografie van de stadsmuren," in *De Witte Raaf* 110 (July–August 2004): 18–21.

13. The very brief intellectual biography in this text is based on two detailed, chronological reconstructions of Lauwaert's life and work by his literary executor Bart Meuleman: Bart Meuleman, "Hoe eenvoudig zou alles niet zijn, mocht ik een taak hebben...," *De Witte Raaf* 171 (September–October 2014): 19–20; and Bart Meuleman, "Kroniek van een afgeladen leven, na de val uit het paradijs," *De Witte Raaf* 191 (January–February 2018): 7–9.

14. Dirk Lauwaert, "Dromen van een expeditie," in *Dromen van een expeditie. Geschriften over film, 1971–2001* (Nijmegen: Uitgeverij Vantilt, 2006): 115.

15. Lauwaert, "Dromen van een expeditie," 114.

16. Lauwaert, "Dromen van een expeditie," 115.

17. Lauwaert, "Berichten uit een klas," 39.

18. Lauwaert, "Dromen van een expeditie," 112.

19. Lauwaert's "committed detachment" is also evident in his preference for the photobook, according to Steven Humblet a constant in his photo criticism: "Not a review of an exhibition but rather of a collection of printed photography. Most of the criticism that appears between 1977 and 1984 (...) deals with one or more photobooks. It says a lot about the exceptional position of printed photography in Lauwaert's thinking. Photography is studied on paper, on the writer's table, where it remains available. Contact with the image occurs while browsing, step by step. Dealing with (printed) photography is a process of looking again and again." Steven Humblet, "'...een catastrofe, een revolutie; een omwenteling.' Dirk Lauwaert over fotografie," *De Witte Raaf* 191 (January–February 2018): 15.

20. Lauwaert, "Hedendaags sofisme en de arme ervaring," 209.

21. Dirk Lauwaert, "Barthes, de perfecte bourgeois," in *Onrust* (Ghent: het balanseer, 2011), 183.

22. Dirk Lauwaert, "Portret van een rol: de intellectueel," in *Onrust* (Ghent: het balanseer, 2011), 88.

23. Peter Delpeut, "Herinneringen aan Dirk Lauwaert," *De Witte Raaf* 192 (March–April 2018): 19–21.

24. "In his articles, he likes to put names in parentheses, as if he were showing his library to you—and expects you to have read it all, too. It is his form of polemic or display of admiration: putting something in parentheses." Peter Delpeut, "Herinneringen aan Dirk Lauwaert," *De Witte Raaf* 192 (March–April 2018): 21.

25. For a historical overview of the beginning of Lauwaert's trajectory in photography criticism, see Steven Humblet, "'...een catastrofe, een revolutie; een omwenteling.' Dirk Lauwaert over fotografie," *De Witte Raaf* 191 (January–February 2018): 15–18.

26. Sometimes Lauwaert does not get around to moving house, farewells, or lost infatuation. Dirk Pültau points to uninhabited and unloved territory in his aperçu of Lauwaert's rejection of the iconoclasm of the avant-garde and of abstract art that wants to (or, according to Lauwaert, thinks it can) wipe clean the slate of the past. Pültau locates Lauwaert's tolerance threshold or "critical boundary" between "abstracting and abstraction. Art's path toward abstraction until Cubism, just before World War I, is affirmed by Lauwaert to be an inevitable outcome of the critique of representation that imposes itself from the mid-nineteenth century onward; after that, he mostly drops out. For him, indeed, it is crucial that art continues to relate to representation, no matter how critical and strained that relation may be." Pültau parries the possible perception of Lauwaert as conservative, reactionary, and antimodernist by specifying one of the cores of his writing: "Any criticism of modernity by Lauwaert—and thus also his rejection of certain modern phenomena or art forms—must be seen in the light of his *obsession* with modernity. Modernity can only be understood if one 'writes through it,' if one contemplates it and *understand its feelings* to its most ambiguous and horrifying (in)consequence while thinking and writing. Hence the pathos in Lauwaert's texts, which is often related to the way in which his fascination turns into dismay. (...)

In this respect, one could call Lauwaert an archaeologist of modernity, were it not for the fact that this formulation sounds too detached and lacks the inextricable knot of fascination and horror that drives his thinking. This critical and pathetic affirmation makes up the basic attitude of Lauwaert's thinking. He does not share the illusory position on modernity so cherished by 'antimodernists.' This is palpable right down to the 'facture' of his texts; his 'writing while thinking,' alternately fractured and spiraling forward or expanding, is marked by the same fragmentation and crumbling that he registers in the crisis of modernity. It makes Lauwaert's critical oeuvre eminently seismographic—permeated by the shocks it brings up." Dirk Pültau, "'Een kunst die nog dialogeert.' Dirk Lauwaert op de drempel van de abstracte kunst," *De Witte Raaf* 192 (March–April 2018): 8 and 7.

27. Lauwaert, "Barthes, de perfecte bourgeois," 174.

28. Lauwaert, "Denken als ritmeren," *Andere Sinema* 110 (July–August 1992): 50.

29. In his dissection of Lauwaert's film criticism, Gerard-Jan Claes states unequivocally that Lauwaert's mode is at odds with the temperament of contemporary film criticism: "Sociological, psychological, or anthropological tendencies and mutations are not read as symptoms in the narrative or ideological framework but are observed within the formal context of the film. Lauwaert's motto is: 'don't explain, but establish, first and foremost.'" Starting from the viewing experience, writing about film does not serve any instruction manual or audience recruiting but rather "the need to invent one's own forms, the desire to remember the film, to repeat it, to recompose it, to reshape it in writing. Not a description or evocation, but a continuation by other means, watching *again* through writing." Gerard-Jan Claes, "Woorden over film. Over Dirk Lauwaerts filmkritiek," *De Witte Raaf* 192 (March–April 2018): 7.

30. Dirk Lauwaert, "De soevereine dandy," in *Onrust* (Ghent: het balanseer, 2011), 154–155.

31. Lauwaert, "Portret van een rol: de intellectueel," 71.

32. Lauwaert, "Portret van een rol: de intellectueel," 81–82.

33. Dirk Lauwaert, "Publiek/publicatie/publiceren/publiciteit," in *Lichtpapier. Teksten over fotografie* (Antwerp: FotoMuseum Provincie Antwerpen, 2007), 131–132.

I

Contemporary Sophistry and the Poor Experience[1]

Where do I end up when I accompany my experiences, when I take them as my guide and provide them with commentary at the same time? Where do I end up when I want to understand them but also be guided by them? I am aware of how perilous that choice is. Questioning myself, I realize how unsteady, how indefinable my experiences are. I realize that experience is a utopia—something you would like to have but may never get. Life as a search for experiences.

I realize that, at the moment, the experience industry is the biggest of all. Today, nothing about my experiences escapes the gaze of universally implemented behaviorism. No experiences, only kicks, are produced here (Lieven De Cauter, *De archeologie van de kick*)[2]. What is a kick for me? An experience reduced to its rhetorical shell. An experience reduced to the advertising of experience. A kick is a McGuffin.

Experience is a multifaceted concept. It marks simultaneously the beginning and the end of life events. Having "an experience" contrasts with having "experience." The former is about punctual impact, the latter is about processing on a deeper and broader level. Experiences are necessary for experience, but experience gets in the way of having experiences. The more experience one has, the harder it becomes to have experiences.

"Experience" is singular, "an experience" is always plural; "one experience" is never enough. Experience, however, is not just the culmination of many experiences. Experience rejects experiences. Those who gain too many experiences for too long, do not reach experience. Experience thus becomes a way of saving on experiences.

The most beautiful aim always seemed to me to be the impossible theory of the concrete, analysis of the subjective, systematics of the sensuous (Roland Barthes in *Fragments d'un discours amoureux* and in *La Chambre claire*).[3] Reflection that does not first neutralize the experiences only to never return to them but is as close as possible to those experiences. *Raisonieren* with my impressions: talking reason into them, allowing myself to be talked round by their reason.

This ultimately means not hardening the work into a document—but trying to grasp it in the moment and form of its appearance. Again, Roland Barthes leads the way. For him, text is a stubborn object of analysis, not a stubborn object of experience.

It means facing the work like a musician playing a score. It can never be the same twice. It is always a new performance. There is always a need for great concentration. Systematics as "performance." Performance as the great model.

Critical reflection is today no longer a subtle performance, a careful interpretation, but a decipherment, an inventorying. A speculative investigation instead of the fragile intimacy of performance. No longer the touch of a hesitant lover but the cut of a coroner. No, I am not surprised that people today refuse reflection on art: they do not consider it, but occupy it. The instrument of that occupation are the humanities.

My small theory of experience stems from artisanal problems. Teaching is "getting to know": each other as a host, bringing them together, proposing a common subject. Because the work is old and came a long way and the student young and untraveled, both have to briefly get into each other's presence. I have to channel them to the same lock for a moment. And the hardest part is providing the students with presence. They already think they are so present in life that nothing more can be added. But it is necessary, for it is useless and therefore pernicious to talk about that strange guest from afar if they are ogling at something behind them.

It escapes the students that my words only belong to the work like a bowl belongs with the fruit, a pedestal under a sculpture, a wooden frame around a photograph: as a means of stirring attention and expressing appreciation. I have to make the students look into the eyes of the work, enabling the "first gaze" that unleashes infatuation.

To make something understandable, you have to make it graspable. Grasping starts with not keeping one's hands to oneself. Around the work, which always comes from afar, immediacy must be constructed. Without that presence, anything you say about the piece of work becomes: information. We all know how useless and, therefore, destructive information is. Information creates absence. Sartre would say it nihilates. Information says: I am telling you something that does not concern you, that you will listen to anyway, but don't worry, it is such that you can immediately forget it.

Information is a vacuum machine. Its great model is photography. It does not connect, it is sterile. This sterility is extraordinarily active.

Those who employ information, do not question its immense, perverse effect, but only its correctness. They do not ask about what is connected by information but whether it has been verified—verification consisting in adducing yet other information. That information must be objective, means that it cannot be related to anything, that the only possible relation is an objectifying antirelation. I no longer even need to be there to receive information: I let it register, I pile it up like dead possessions. Computer memories really serve a purpose, namely that I could be absent.

My small belief in experience also stems from some encounters with the academic world. Some but they were traumatizing. In the literal sense of the word: something that makes you fundamentally uncertain; a wound that structures your further doings (a way of being born or launched on a path you can't leave). The traumatized set up camp around the trauma; what they do and think is an adverse homage to that trauma. Precisely because it was so threatening, it will never let go (Marc Nacht, *À l'aise dans la barbarie*).[4]

What was that trauma? It was the outrageous ambition to know without experience. Emblematic in my history are the historian who saw no need to see the films he was studying, the art historian who never had an opinion on the work, and the theorist who branded the "amateur" as a hysteric.

The permanent war of the clerks of any culture against the aesthetic, more specifically against the touch that moves one in unpredictable ways. Today's managers and yesterday's revolutionaries are scared to death of that touch, but both exploit it to snare others.

Experience is earthly, banal and disenchantingly concrete (it is also compelling, unreasonable and easily hysterical). Experience fetters you between these two poles—between disenchantment and hysteria. Not a pure, not a clean, not a peaceful situation. Something that balances between cursing and poetry; something like vomiting pearls. But I do find that earthly and hysterical unreasonableness of experience tantalizing. That is when the real work begins. So as to cure ourselves of the mannerism of our intellectuality, of the distorting mirror held up to us as "true" during this carnival "because" everything is false anyway, as everything is rhetoric. From Régis Debray[5] to Leo De Haes,[6] along very different lines, it nevertheless always comes down to the fact that we should draw comfort and strength from deceit and bad taste. *Vive les corrupteurs, puisqu'il n'y a que de la corruption.* [Long live the corrupters, since there is only corruption.] Trompe l'oeil thinking dominates our time.

Experience is not the opposite of reflection, it demands reflection. Without experience as a distant but ever-present pole, there is no reason to reflect. Isn't reflection always triggered by the shocking and astonishing subjugation at the heart of our sense of "self" and "autonomy"? Does not this very paradoxical unfree freedom force us to think?

Is thinking a freer alternative to the risk of our unfree experiences? Alas, thinking left to itself immediately becomes "having to think." Experience points to something else, but words are more convincing. Thinking is immediately what you have to think (after all, thinking provides convincing evidence), but especially what you can no longer think afterwards. The "what you have to do" has been replaced with "what you can't do anymore." Thinking's pedantic, admonishing rule of propriety. Who would have thought thinking so deeply conformist? Oh, the nuisance of constantly hearing people and reading texts that want to curtail my library again!

Reflection only barely endures experience, as an uneducated and moody creature. Experience is so exasperating simply because it is what it is: obscenely old-fashioned, banally reactionary, absolutely naive, shameful in its choices, but so grandiosely indisputable. (Not unlike a crush, or a friendship that is beyond arguments.)

That wonderful unreasonableness and unruliness of experience! That which escapes order. It is certainly not thinking that will undermine order. This much is clear to me today after half a century of living. Thinking is always so obedient! Never trust reflection! (Pay attention to adjectives; read about substantives!)

Experience is supposed to be clear; a way of getting to the core things. Experience is fundamentally without detours and doubts. These always come afterwards and have to be removed. Experience is a fiercely materialistic ideal. An ideal when you realize you have no time to waste with speculations. Experiences are quick, immediate and, therefore, never distracted (that silly proposal by Benjamin!).

Today, people argue in favor of, develop skills for, and create a climate that justifies insensitivity. First step: teaching distrust. Those famous new media are nothing but a technique of insensitization (sensitization was a term of the old media!).

It is not a coincidence that there is no experiential critique of the new media. Even *Andere Sinema*,[7] the theoretical organ of the new media par excellence, does not offer experiential critique. Because it is impossible, I suppose, as the new media do not mediate experience. The curious thing is that people are not surprised by that impossibility but on the contrary seem to welcome it. There is only hysterical theory about it.

What else are the humanities today, with their fastening upon culture, corporeality, visuality, etc., but incubators of endless sophistry? (One day the humanities will be judged.)

When will this wave of intellectual mannerism blow over? How else is Paul De Vylder's work, for instance, to be understood?[8] Surely this is a pretentious course in "visual language" which dismisses any emotion as a fraud. A brutal operation without tact, without elegance, but above all without vitality. Right from the start, whatever the work aims to make clear is worthless to me, because the idea of the image has been castrated in advance. Whoever first ridicules the image and promises the spectator such immense superiority is fighting a battle they cannot lose. A pose, therefore, and a technique. Something that exists only in the false problems it wants to talk us into. This critique of kitsch is itself Homerically kitschy (that is to say blind to its own ridiculousness).

Young students today look at photographs and their "impact," at films and how "efficient" they are, and art aficionados look at art and how "interesting" it is. Interesting is the death sentence of experience. An interesting experience is a perverse contradiction in terms. An experience cannot yield "interest." An experience is not functional, but compelling, disruptive, exhausting, extreme. Experience is the way in which the unknown—which today is the inappropriately banal, the extremely obvious—challenges you. Experience is incompatible with economic return. An "interesting" experience is a devaluation of experience to a means.

Experience doesn't fit in a system of progress. One does not capitalize on experience. A tree that grows is not a tree that makes progress. We have lost that motif of growth as a paradigm. With the learning outcomes, it is even banned from our reflection on education, or more accurately, perverted. This motif of growth has to do with the belief that is part and parcel of trust. To see a tree grow is to believe in the continuity of its transformation. What to do with this observation when our greatest intellectual sport is the phantom battle with identity?

What are we to make of that trust when Magritte is for us the ultimate revelation about the image! Do we really think the history of the image is nothing but the illusion Magritte plays with? How much we apparently hate our imagination. How we like to delude ourselves into thinking we are victims of the image and now need postmodern therapy. What a pseudo-lesson!

Experiences miraculously become "my experience," like knowledge becomes insight, like a culture crystallizes into a repertoire with which we are bound up as fundamentally as with our own names. It is—of course—as arbitrary as it is inescapable. Indeterminate here does not mean indiscriminately exchangeable. And inescapability here is not a yoke but the only possibility, the only chance we get. The repertoire is not a hit parade, not a manipulable code.

By turning art into culture, however, the code seems to have been installed. We are dealing with a collection in an enumeration, a collection in a vault (that of the academy, the bank, the government, a database, an encyclopedia). Therefore, the relationship between the beholder and the work today favors the objectifying beholder, to the detriment of the object. We are focused on manipulation and rhetoric. Being aesthetically overwhelmed is an outdated game, replaced by bluff and provocation.

It is clear, today the aesthetic is irritating, for aesthetic human beings find themselves in an unflattering position: they are passive and essentially naive. In this imperial age, the ironic view of the world is our lot, as if the world itself were an advertising slogan of the Kosmos company. Against art, we wage a colonialist war of liberation (excuse the oxymoron).

Maybe every experience is an illusion. I look at photographs but do I experience them? I often have the feeling that no real experience of photographs is possible, only kicks and vague impressions. It really confuses me at times. Photographs have that traumatizing force that nothing can get between. Photographs are—unlike the fragments of the world that can be seen in them—fundamentally unpoetic.

In fact, such depoetization happens to everything that is copied and comes to us by relay. Loss of aura, Benjamin diagnosed, but above all a loss of experience. That which is reproduced is by definition abundance—which homeostatically evokes the poverty of experience.

Experience is the color and smell the world has for us.

Experience is fundamentally obstinate toward the word, toward commentary. Especially toward methodical, ordered commentary, which forces (must force) the discussed subject into the straitjacket of its starting point. Experience explodes that language, lures thinking away from itself, on several paths at once, in a contradictory and paradoxical way. Hence another language strategy, that of criticism in the form of poetry: didactic poems. Not the expression of emotions or events, but the struggle to see and know, as close to experience as possible.

Experience introduces the "standpoint" (for an experience, you have to stand somewhere). From there, things can be viewed, approached, judged, valued. Experience is a point of view: it installs in the universe the incarnational principle "from where." Experience is never omniscient (of which objective is a derivative) but always knowing "as" or "to the extent that": angle, approach, focus, point of view.

The standpoint allows experience to introduce the possibility of "valuing." Valorization is nuanced, modulated distance. Value creation and standpoints are one and the same. Without experience, no criticism is possible. (The fading away of criticism is the fading out of the standpoint.) When everything becomes a product, one loses the possibility of a standpoint.

Experience injects a moral principle into the aesthetic. A principle that replaces the exterior authority of tradition and assignment. Experience has to do with authenticity, an elated concept that pairs up with the ironic critique of authenticity.

Wouldn't there be a third way? Couldn't we conceive of a wisdom of experience: one that acknowledges its relativity but does not experience that relativity as offensive, that experiences this inescapable relativity as a duty and not a right (expressionism).

Experience is the bourgeois creation par excellence, the core from which religion, science, politics, and art were recalibrated. Experience is a bourgeois concept that people want to eradicate today. With good reasons:

experience is the principle of "resistance" par excellence. Experience is at the heart of the principle of "autonomy."

The aesthetic experience has long aspired to be the locus of the shocking experience, of revelation and wonder. Ever since critical culture, that has been its raison d'être. Today, that role of experience is played out. It used to be the fact that experience was not progressive; today experience is reputed to be tainted with too much "belief."

Both experience and insight are threatened, eroded, and destroyed by exposition. A certain way of showing is blinding. Everyone knows and feels this destruction. How could the devastation of the world not have a destructive counterpart elsewhere?

That which would have been denounced two decades ago is cynically applauded today—by the same generation!—in accordance with the adage that keeps on coming true in this century: what is, must be. Isn't that what Leo De Haes's realism in, say, *Het doemdenken voorbij* boils down to, the perfect mirror image of that other dubious activity, the utopia that says: what is, must disappear. Yesterday's utopians are forever tomorrow's narrow-minded *Real*-moralists. Both are accomplices of power and its histrionics.

Art, intellectuality, media—they are no longer a critical mirror of what really exists but the death mask of power sucking up all that exists. Media and advertising are preeminent instruments for extending power, that is, for making us take part in power even more, that is, for letting power corrupt us and make us disappear. There is nothing in that dead vacuum of power. That nothingness needs to be nurtured. That is why we must take part in power. Any artistic expression, any medium today is caught up in the false illusion of being able to pull power to one's own side.

The disappearance of experience is the triumph of power. Power causes experience to evaporate. We are all taking part in that power, ever more intimately. How to escape it without lapsing into a political act? How to keep the door closed to the specter of power? How to step out of a society in which power seems to have spread everywhere?

The secularization of the world and of art and of intellectual life is not its objectification into knowledge but a fatal grab for power. Power is a Commendatore. Experience is Don Juan. Our art today is no longer an homage to the man of passions, but to the cold Commendatore.[9]

Reports from a Classroom[1]

The most puzzling to me is still that they sit waiting for me in the morning. Why are they sitting there? They never tell me. I "teach" them to the best of my ability. They stay seated, don't run away, don't throw anything at me, they listen. Often bored, sometimes alert; often tired, sometimes awake. The question lingers on but gradually takes on a new form. What exactly do they hear when they listen to me (the most peculiar things, as it turns out)?

Better to give shape and substance to that assignment myself (I think it is useful "for that," I reassure myself). After this, the dust cloud of considerations that slowly settles into you like a *main courante* with which you start the descent into that unknowable other. I realize that my struggle with the compelling as well as unmeetable demand for something to hold on to is the verse to which a teacher's thorny path is scanned. As long as I myself know why and how I stand there. But do I? I take a deep breath before opening the classroom door.

1.

Teaching is vaudeville: a farce in which the blindfolded teacher chases dozens of ruthless students. From both sides, the only certainty is misunderstanding. The comedy of generations is given one last chance here, after the family, to manifest itself in all its glory. *Der Blaue Engel* delineates the fundamental fate of all teachers. We are all slightly pompous. We owe that to our status. It shields us, too (we think).

Pedagogy is the continuation of paternal (parental) relationships, expectations, illusions, impasses, and triumphs. Thinking about teaching (and being taught) is best done in those terms, within that same field of tension. You suddenly see the extreme fragility and intimacy of what happens in this relationship; the impalpable complexity of the process emerges. This is not only a flow of knowledge and information, but rather a flow of expectations, images, projections. Teachers' investment in their students mimics the identifications and bonds of parents with their children.

2.

That is, at least, how I fare: I love sitting at a school desk myself and listening to people for whom something exists *as thought*. Learning (as thinking) is not an exasperating disgrace but an absolute delight.

What's more: I realize that this listening happens within the order of the spectacle. The audience that came to listen to Kraus, Bergson, or Foucault[2] were attending a worship: the cruel theatre of ideas. Thought exists *as spectacle*.

Thinking is an activity that follows an aesthetic pattern. That aesthetic aspect is less trivial and misplaced than it seems. After all, it concerns the manner of addressing, the way in which one conveys the importance of the object under study. That form must be tailored, beautiful, convincing, elegant, and subtle. Knowledge always has to do with style: the way in which one creates and perpetuates knowledge. Because it is so rare, an insight is too precious just to hand it out in a dirty wrapper.

But you also notice that the aesthetic attention to form touches the very core of thinking, because thinking has everything to do with form. The question of whether knowledge is beautiful, convincing, and stimulating turns out not to be alien to that knowledge. Such questions stimulate the understanding of your subject matter, rather than needlessly burdening it. As it turns out, the aesthetic question is an eminent knowledge question.

3.

Teaching has to do with demonstration and example. This presupposes a radical break between those who demonstrate and those who watch. Those who demonstrate, put themselves on display, make themselves available; they are models on which something is tested. Those who watch closely here are witnesses to a peculiar process; something of the order of offering. Someone offers himself as an example. He makes himself transparent, accessible. He gives a rendition of his own contours, as precisely and sharply as possible. The other can look with impunity in every possible way: a cruel spectacle, with a model that very quickly shrivels into a caricature, no longer existing for himself but solely for the other. He is doomed to an actor's fate. Isn't this caricature what we later remember about the teacher? A caricature after mastering what has been taught.

The teacher who offers himself as an example, however, has no power over the image the onlooker forms of him. This distinguishes teachers from actors. The one who offers himself as an example does not put on a show; if anything, he reveals his secrets. He is well aware, and so is the student—even though both pretend not to know about each other. Without this, all this would be impossible. He knows he is protected by the blindness with which he strikes his listeners, precisely by making himself visible as an example. He knows (he hopes) that he is elsewhere than where his listeners think him to be. He hopes to be hidden in his visibility (an illusion nonetheless).

4.

To teach is to pass on, to say that no one begins with themselves, that everyone continues. Language is given; so is knowledge. It is a knowing that one does not make oneself, but that one carries in that endless line of transference. An inheritance of questions and ways of thinking of which one is the recipient, not the origin. Knowledge comes from elsewhere, like culture. That idea of transference, of investiture seems so essential to me. That is what makes learning so different from the great competing system called Information and Communication.

Pedagogy is both power over the future and preservation of the past, over which one equally claims power. Pedagogy is preservation. When "topicality" competes with the past and the future ever more efficiently, pedagogy becomes jeopardized.

Learning has to do with wisdom; but we—children of our history—think it has to do with progress. For instance, we are so keen on "critical" education! But criticism and wisdom rarely go together; in a certain way, they are even radically incompatible. The subject matter of criticism is topicality; wisdom withdraws from it.

The critical mind ultimately needs the object of its criticism more than its victory over it. The critical mind does not condemn (it just seems that way). It rather takes possession—in its own way, of course, negatively. Wisdom, on the other hand, has to do with detachment; especially from that which annoys.

5.

Education is big business. It is the crucial apparatus of the ideological exertion of power. It is an institution, a bureaucracy. Subject to all the evils and pressures of big state enterprises.

The language it speaks—with those much vaunted learning outcomes, for instance, is a mixture of moralization and bureaucratization, of content and controllability. It is a turnkey transfer of the entire state apparatus to the inevitable next step: not only the reorganization of personnel, but also the reorganization of ideas. Any transparency (who could object to that? only those who have something to hide) leads irrevocably to trivialization as well as hypocrisy. Transparency has perverse side effects.

The less one thinks in terms of engagement and the more in terms of return, the more unattainable the secret of teaching becomes.

Learning has no program—it is a process fraught with inevitable, necessary imponderables. Programs obscure that fact. Programs can do no harm, as long as one remains aware of that fact; but programs are there, of course, to avert that awareness.

Programs are also—that's how it goes—beginning to look more and more like their machine versions. Processable by a computer—the household appliance installing bureaucracy *chez soi* everywhere.

The language of learning outcomes: catastrophic for its sterile neutrality; suggesting a utopia of outcomes made equal by machines. Life courses reduced to accounting sums and differences. Above all, the elimination of risk (of abuse, incompetence, injustice). Bureaucracy sweats out the paper people's distrust of everyone else: that exasperatingly uncontrollable liveliness that keeps creating ways through which the result cannot be entered and justified accounting-wise. So much control is asking for punitive abuse.

6.

The most important thing falls outside the realm of learning and teaching, namely, experience: that which addresses you exclusively and profoundly changes you. The appeal is unique, once only, unplannable: ultimately of the order of epiphany, of "grace," of the undeserved "gift."

Work needs to be done to restore the capacity for experience, and the realization that ultimately things are not compulsory (not available) but possible, in short, cannot be enforced.

We are quick to experience such a state as impermissible because it forces us to admit that there is no causal connection between effort and result. Education, then, is no longer a procedure with imperative necessity according to a natural law. There is not even a psychological or mental law. Experience as a result is unenforceable. Knowledge and skill and information, however, very much are.

Education is a very porous structure of society; it is being quietly eroded by the surrounding commodity thinking. The same intolerable plannability that all the media and consultants recommend to us.

It is important to safeguard a space in which the revolutions of big experiences can take place. It is supposed to be a secret, inaccessible space. The learning process "around it" has no right of access there, on pain of depriving that space of its very potential.

7.

My question about experience has to do with the fear that experience loses quality, is affected by a much simpler proposition, that of exposition.

Show and you will understand, *look* and you will also have seen. It is about the restless knowability of things, the demand for unlimited learnability for all. Reduce everything to culture (to the banal obviousness of "these are my surroundings") and you are left with a world that exists only insofar as it is visible to all. A progressive disenchantment, which of course is also a progressive *liberation* (after all, disenchantment is liberating).

Democratization means devaluation. Democratization is the prohibition of initiation. But without initiation, that is, the effort needed to make a choice, to take sides, any domain is lost in banal self-evidence. Initiation provides mystery, a path towards it, projects an object and your relationship with it into a time sequence, turns it into a story, brings it into relief. Consumption is the denial of any relief in favor of an even equality of things, in favor of distanceless obviousness.

Perhaps (true) culture is the magnified and objectified fight between the disenchantment of the world into an object and the necessary reenchantment of the world as experience. A process that plays out in every individual as one of the stakes of existence (the fight against cynicism), but which is increasingly also a fight in the public arena. Education is an important link in this regard.

8.

(*Isn't he known for working theoretically?*) In fact, his only concern in teaching is to *make something exist*: a photograph, a film sequence, a style, a thought, a way of questioning things, the power with which an idea is posited in a text, an image, a sequence of images. Here, he would like to use the word "contemplate," which includes the sensory "to see" but especially the mental "to inspect": to verify. Looking and considering whether and how something is.

(*Theory has increasingly proven to him to be an accomplice of absence.*) In fact, it is not something he pursues: surely everyone can verify whether something exists. But he himself doubts that. He doesn't see it in the statements, nor in the pupils of his listeners. Their ever-sluggish postures deny that something new has suddenly come to join them that morning.

9.

With words, he tries to temper the deafening noise of the silent presence of an image. While speaking, he conjures it, welcomes it, gives it a place, so that it can become attached, leave traces. While speaking, he photographs that miraculous appearance, which placidly endures his words. Thus, in language, he hopes to have found for himself and others a mnemonic means by which to prove how and that there has been experience of something.

He is quietly convinced that we function more and more in terms of sensation and information, less and less in terms of experience. In information and sensation, there is a bad form of presence (too low, too high). That is how experience falls into disuse. Yet only experience allows you to know undeniably that something exists. All other forms are instrumental: mediating, indirect, subject to all manipulations along the way.

Again and again, he wonders dispiritedly if he has found the right word, the right dosage, the right silence for offering to the surrounding demagogy the haughty defense of keeping still. Is his irony not a source of misunderstanding, his indignation too easy, his self-doubts too precious, his purpose as problematic as it is misplaced? But what else could his task be, other than to teach eyes to breathe, to give rhythm to consciousness, to make both susceptible to what really comes from outside and to briefly withdraw both eyes and consciousness from gravity. But he often feels like Rebecca Horn's butterflies: lyrical and mechanical at the same time, flying and programmed. But, he then thinks, that is our painful form of presence: the crippling combinations of the most intimate feeling and a machine, of presence and crutches to give it existence.[3]

Critique of Enthusiasm

Culture, or the Event; The Accompanying Word: Passion[1]

"Passion"—as the logic of the event prescribes—is always deployed in an inclusive way. "Passion" unites. But passion and enthusiasm are divisive, they exclude. The access ban is essential. Worthy of its ambitions, enthusiasm is elitist, not democratic, precisely not an accomplice of the participatory. Later, in the inevitable reckoning, that refusal is invariably branded as snobbery.

Enthusiasm is belief, confession. It implies responsibility, commitment. As such, enthusiasm is, if not frightening, disturbing. Enthusiasm makes for confusion, not confirmation. What cruel enthusiasm.

It's true, enthusiasm does not have a clean soul. The twentieth century burned out on enthusiasm. Too little self-criticism, and no moderating self-discipline, no ability to correctly determine its place in the world and life: this way, enthusiasm becomes a plaything instead of leaven. Vulgar instead of refined. Elitist in ambition, plebeian in form. (Appreciation of enthusiasm is recent, an effect of the Enlightenment. Until then, enthusiasm was suspect and heretical, order-disturbing.)

Besides, its loud and polemical character silences an underlying uncertainty. Part of the appeal of enthusiasm is the overcoming of that uncertainty. A source of courage, of hubris, a driving force for collecting arguments, checking details, developing knowledge, and exploring modes of knowledge. Enthusiasm generates knowledge and method. One loves not only the object of enthusiasm but also the enthusiasm itself that gives birth to intellectual vitality.

Then again: what is a life against enthusiasm? Whining, whittling down, footnoting. How much jealousy zeal calls into being. Proud enthusiasm must be destroyed, the fire extinguished, the shining armor "matted" in mud. Who wants a new beginning? There are so many reasons to brush off enthusiasm. But are they good reasons? To enthusiasm's credit is its capacity for reviving, for pushing the boundaries of the world. With enthusiasm, the world becomes larger; without it, it shrivels, or worse still, it falls apart.

Passionate love, the fiery breath of enthusiasm or the moral necessity of commitment gives access to a unique spiritual adventure. Without it, one takes note of something, stores information about it, names its effect, not its meaning, not its ability to change someone's world, to offer a view on yet another way of existing in the world. Enthusiasm is nothing but the will to change. This is possible only when one engages radically with the object. When one throws oneself into the movement of the work. When one places oneself such that there is no escape.

In enthusiasm, the drive takes over from the mind. Enthusiasm is, by definition, unreasonable. The literary form par excellence of enthusiasm is the critical commentary (the small version of the essay): pointed, attacking, dense. Speed is its condition. It is menacing. Intellectual guerrilla. Not the rightness of proof or the rightness of lawyers, but the rightness of surviving, of making enthusiasm itself survive. Enthusiasm is an existential plea.

Enthusiasm translates thinking into a drive. But it is a chaste drive. Enthusiasm sublimates. It is not desire (like that of a collector) but a tribute at a distance. That which arouses enthusiasm becomes at once untouchable. The enthusiast is the vestal virgin of a service. The "nearness" of enthusiasm is a parade: it is ultimately about distance, about detachment. In that sense, enthusiasm is always also moralizing. The ever-young enthusiasm does not know the skin of things. Enthusiasm is not erotic.

That is why enthusiasm so often carries friendships. It is the sublimating mediator. Enthusiasm is male and same-sex. It is a postponement of life, a diversion, an antechamber before entering life. Enthusiasm is not a female passion, and not part of marriage. Between lovers, enthusiasm gets in the way. Enthusiasm is celibate.

Enthusiasm has a double relation to time: enthusiasm always seems to be a snapshot, in the present. But it always comes immediately after (the comment: "did you see that?") and affirms an unbroken future ("this is forever"). Imperfect, present, and imperative. Not the past experience nor the future plan but the now as both a past and a future without change (the structure of a confession of faith). The rhythm of enthusiasm is the gallop. Its figure of speech, the leap over a hurdle. The leap as a tribute.

Enthusiasm leaves only burned bridges, considers itself the Future pure and simple. Enthusiasm then appears as the project for a nomadic existence. The essence of the enthusiastic gallop is irrevocable wandering. The enthusiast as a mental drifter. The passion of enthusiasm is pathetic. Enthusiasm is repulsive. It is no different in religion, as people already knew in the past: heretics lead a wandering existence (*L'Oeuvre au noir*).

Enthusiasm is not just an ability bestowed upon a person; it also depends on specific conditions that permit, generate, compel enthusiasm. Enthusiasm is also and perhaps above all the gift of a zeitgeist. Some (I suspect very exceptional) periods allow enthusiasm, thriving on it, presupposing it. Apart from that: the easy pleasure of consumption, that is, of what is for granted.

Change, turnover, and revolution are conditions for enthusiasm (enthusiasm enables them, blinds them too). Besides "there is a revolution going on" also "this revolution must be." Indignation, resentment, destructiveness, and war campaigns are part of this enthusiastic passion. No generation of the twentieth century escaped the happiness but also the fate of enthusiasm. How does one escape the exhaustion of enthusiasm, its inherent fragility, its shameful unreasonableness, its fallacies and virtuosity, which only the young and inexperienced are able to cope with? How to escape its compulsion, its neurosis, its sublimation?

One: simply ignore the enthusiasm. Today we see that not only people but an entire culture is possible without enthusiasm. A culture with events but without euphoria. A culture that is a direct and all too accommodating object of power. A culture that sits at the table with power. Admittedly, being an accomplice of power is traditionally culture's self-evident, natural, only role. And yet, without a sovereign and after today's enthusiasm, it feels quite different, this complicity with power. Rubbing up against the inclusive ideal of media and consumption is different from providing royalty and church with images. The latter have ambitions. Do the former have any?

In a strategic culture, taking up a position does not imply commitment but calculation, not risk but the averting of it. Discoveries here are of a very different order than those that fall to enthusiasm's share. The disturbing ideal of enthusiasm as an exhausting nocturnal gallop was replaced with the ideal of the network (a wondrous combination of movement and being stuck).

The network may allow discoveries but they are of an entirely different order from those of the last century. Its snobbery is not elitist but populist-hued. Against the ukase of enthusiasm, an elimination race. No longer the tribunal but the forum, no longer the trial but the poll. Not passion but a warm-up comedian. A somewhat dull but efficient alternative to overly cruel enthusiasm.

To be left behind by enthusiasm is to hang on to it for dear life: nagging nostalgia, alienation from that which presents itself as novel, retrospective idealization of enthusiasm. This is not a step out of enthusiasm but its ossification. The reckless "rightness" of enthusiasm turning into a "wrongedness" of disappointment.

Yet nostalgia may turn out to be a continuation of enthusiasm: Late Enthusiasm. This is always a tricky exercise: does "Late" denote decay or the absolute peak? Is that peak accumulation or purification? Excess, as in Late-Renaissance Mannerism, or ultimate synthesis, as in Matisse's cutouts? What could be the contours of someone's Late Enthusiasm?

It helps to realize that even in its heyday, enthusiasm looks for predecessors and does not think of itself as simply new. The gaze ahead of enthusiasm searches the past for accomplices, father figures, seducers. Every innovation seeks an investiture of the past. André Breton plundered the past like no other. Especially those who reach for the future, seek a right that they will never find among contemporaries and therefore seek in the past. The search for predecessors is always *de mauvaise foi* [in bad faith], it is always improper use. It is nostalgia for a past that is not the past of the enthusiast.

Late Enthusiasm can be a similarly ambiguous option: for instance, enthusiastic criticism of enthusiasm. At once inside and outside, at once a putting into perspective and a triumphant rightness (but it just as easily admits it is in the wrong). The heyday of enthusiasm as a testator one abuses and continues to give life. What comes after enthusiasm as vital nostalgia.

The classic is a possible result of the reflection on and the distance from enthusiasm. After the imprudence and brutality of High Enthusiasm, the caution of Late Verification. What remains after the frenzy? What remains of the battlefield of the first, young, virile enthusiasm? A wealth of suggestions and proposals to be pruned. Dying off and repelled into the mass grave. The annoying thing (from the standpoint of enthusiasm) is all too easy rightness. The classic settles the accounts in order to establish a canon, to trace out reference values as foundations for a stable world, for an order (westerns are built on those same contradictions).

The imaginary genealogy of the enthusingly new is precisely not the establishment of a compulsory canon but the search for accomplices. Moderns are always sons in search of the inspiring father: from inspiration to norm.

Then again, what makes the classic so human is its sublimated nostalgia. The ideal is always already past, it never arrives. Naive enthusiasm relies on the makeable future. The strict law of the classic is a sad law. No one shows this more clearly than Poussin, the classic painter par excellence. He is not the canon that Colbert's doctrinal royal academy wanted to use him for. His series of Sacraments, Seasons, Metamorphoses and religious Passions are told with the obscene pathos of gaping mouths, frenzied glances, wide-open arms and legs, onrushing sprints in tunics like flags in a hurricane. Excessive violence, fuel for zeal and passion. But he stylizes all these movements and expressions into poses, masks, stone-heavy flapping. The classic here raises enthusiasm more highly than ever, but is able to control it less than ever. The classic here is the continuation of kindling enthusiasm, but then in the guise of its bleakest opposite (which is all that Baudelaire did, all that Manet wanted).

In constructing a genealogy for the enthusing, zeal shifts into admiration. Not identification with the strict law but with the nurturing, protective father. Admiration is no longer nomadic; one admires from a more-fixed point. Museums are made for that admiration. Looking up: *di sotto in sù*. That which is admired is not a norm but a call for protection (Anchises[2]). In admiration one does not undergo the law but supports its ruin. Admiration is not discovery but rehabilitation and therefore fidelity.

While enthusiasm is hungry, voracious, cruel, bloodthirsty, insolent and obscene, admiration, on the other hand, is cautious, distant, considerate. The verb "must," inherent in enthusiasm and the classic, does not fit admiration (one may admire, one can admire).

The words of admiration are: finally, still, all things considered. They refer to closure and conclusion, not to a project. Nor does one imitate what one admires. The admired is not a model. On the contrary, the son's admiration does not pursue an imitation of the father. The admired is not imitable, because it is not a law. One accepts the admired, one does not undergo it. Enthusiasm does not have this modesty. This very modesty is the flaw of admiration: one can admire without knowing. The admired as doxa, as cultural myth, swallowed up by consumption (Barthes).

While the museum is the natural home of admiration (any space where there is admiration is a museum), home is the place of emotion (where there is emotion, there is a home). Neither enthusiasm, nor the classic, nor admiration have room for emotion. It is there, probably, but it does not play an establishing role in their trajectory. What comes after enthusiasm, after passion, after admiration? At best, it's this: emotion.

Like enthusiasm and admiration, emotion has an ideal space, its own temporal form, its own gestures. Enthusiasm is theatrical and aches for applause, collectivity, marching. Admiration is a visual projection and demands silence and standstill. Admiration elevates, giving the vertical a passionate substance. Emotion is intimate and demands a home. Its gesture: hands held before the eyes. Its sense is aural. One needs to hear the intimacy of the work. Emotion, or music.

The house is the place without change: in the house one shelters from change. The house keeps out change. Every change threatens the fragile balance of happiness and drama, of memory and survival, of repetition and the surprising gift.

The place of emotion is the wall of the home, far removed from the coldness of the museum hall, from the grandeur of the theater. Emotion is found among memories. A house is the necropolis of private life, growing ever thicker. The objects there have an Andersen-fairytale life rather than a Proust-novel one. Less the object of perception than of magic (Benjamin). In between, some artworks as a countermovement, so as to let the necropolis breathe, to give a signature of its own to the terrible anonymity of memories (everyone remembers the same thing). The objects from the past that one drags along and to which one ascribes a magical power are put out of action by the artwork with a style. Intimacy discharges the necessity of choice; the artwork in the midst of intimacy affirms that life is a choice too. Emotion has less to do with remembering than with that choice, with the tension between the two: life as a project embedded in life as a choice once made, a choice that can't be undone. Emotion radicalizes the work of remembering: here and now, this could have been the situation, but here and now one sees the inexorable shadow of the life choice once made.

In the struggle with memory, the manifesto of enthusiasm, the law of the classic, the certainties of admiration do not help. The "must" no longer helps; in intimacy it is about "can." What can I live with? What can I recognize myself in? What can I still do amid the lapidary of what has already been lived? With what can I go on living, is the question of the good life. The house of emotion is not an escape from the world, but a critique of the world.

The poignant as that which brings you home after a long odyssey: "So that's it." Not a call, but a constatation. Sober and without aspiration. After the great museum hall, after the inexorable white cube of the moderns: Vuillard's screen, Marthe's bathroom,[3] Van Rijsselberge's doorframe, Hammershøi's see-through, Johan Deloore's open window.[4] Moments of the inactual.

The time of emotion is not that of admiration (*la longue durée*) or that of enthusiasm (*l'instantané*) but the time of the work itself. Emotion accompanies the movement of an actor, a melody, a phrase, an enjambment. Not violent, not lasting, but accompanying. Emotion is time that one makes one's own along with the unfolding work. A time that cannot be shared (again that separation). One is always moved alone.

In emotion, the voice skips, the body shaking along in tears. In short, whoever is moved stumbles, clumsiness taking the place of control. Whoever is moved blushes, stutters—comical *maladresse*. Emotion is just that: losing control. With every emotion, a pinch of shame.

While other passionate investments in the work of art always want to be named and justified, emotion recognizes that justification is defense, not candid confession. Emotion wears the mask of a certain stupidity and, why not, a certain tastelessness. The incessant modern critique of the intimate (so different from its creation and exaltation by the Enlightenment). Intimacy is the enemy of modernity, the denial of enthusiasm.

Just as there is a world without enthusiasm, so there is a world without emotion. The critique of kitsch is the crusade against emotion. And that crusade is waged with the greatest enthusiasm. Enthusiasm and emotion are two extremes in line with each other but they are also antipodes. Just as the enthusiastic does not want emotion, so emotion fends off enthusiasm.

Emotion is not principled and strict, but compliant, forgiving, self-willed, radically autonomous: the collective "we" replaced with a private "mine." Emotion is not smart, not self-critical, not seeking recognition. It is not accountable. Does not reconcile itself to norms. On the contrary, that which lets itself be guided by norms rarely moves. In emotion there are no longer any motives, but there is completion. Whoever is moved says: this is finished. Whoever weeps says: this is the limit of what can be experienced. Whoever is moved is like Moses before the Promised Land—there it is, though unattainable. There it is, because it is unattainable. There it is, and therefore it is unattainable. There it is, and luckily it is unattainable. Right there, in that spot, in that realization, there is emotion.

II

Barthes, the Perfect Bourgeois[1]

One does not write about Barthes[2] but along with him. One does not put oneself outside of him but adopts his forms, even if one does not share his arguments. He commands an irresistible form of mimetism. Thinking here inevitably takes the form of a relationship. With him, intellectual labor is always a labor of love. More than anybody else, he reveals the seductive rather than the rhetorical dimension of intellectual life. To accept his figure is to be his partner on the dance floor: he leads, I follow. Nothing is more delightful. He is the Astaire among intellectuals.

Yet later one wonders what the loss of all reserve was all about. Yes, he is fascinating, but perhaps because he himself is not fascinated—as one definition of the Dandy goes. My fascination has to do with his aloofness.

Barthes comes after the generation of commitment; he tries noncommitment. This has been repeatedly described as *déplacement*—at once a theoretical operation and a moral attitude. He is emphatically not looking for the alternative but extracts the inconspicuous place aside. Tilting is his basic operation. Like the leading partner introducing a surprising step, to which you react with delight. Tilting is precisely not a "revolution"—it is not about reversing but about turning. Small and crucial.

Barthes belongs to the generation of distrust. It is clear that there is more about the tilting. The aesthetic of displacement is fueled by a deep panic. The essence of oneself must be held in reserve. Here one does not say "I"—except as an empty *shifter* that has no referent, only a use.

The *shifter*'s emptiness is the utopian point to which he keeps hoping to reduce everything. Meaning not as reference but as a phenomenon of condensation: a shiny deposit on the smoothest surface.

Infatuation is such an ideal, empty figure—it produces "I" and "you," but without motivation, that is, without referent. In the small, catastrophic tilting of infatuation, one is extremely oneself because one is extremely alienated. The infatuated no longer have anything to do with themselves, for they are completely engrossed in a second alienation at the object of their infatuation, which disintegrates into innumerable details.

Tilt and distrust. That is the parade of infatuation that makes me infatuated: with his ideas, language, his rhythm, and attitude to life. I am infatuated, but with whom? Not with someone who is himself infatuated. Does he like photography? I'm sure he doesn't. Balzac? He plays a game with an object. Fashion? He reduces it to text. He does love gestures on stage and at the piano. Perhaps the obscene and at the same time veiled language of postures is what touches him most. Phantasmatically intense gestures unremittingly slide like glowing lava beneath distinguished phrases. Gestures of the dancer, gestures of the infatuated. They are not a language, not an expression but pure matter, as absolute as a dream or obscenity. There is no response to it, no conversation with it: it is there, large as life, tolerating no contradiction.

Intellectual gestures especially take on an overwhelming importance. *Déplacement* is first and foremost just that: less a productive act than a theatricalized gesture. The small displacement does not generate a spectacular new insight but has a great "symbolic" impact. His thinking aims to manifest itself primarily as effect, much less—or precisely not—as productive.

Barthes's work is intensely decorative. Decoration is a way of offering space, objects, images and trajectories: decoration is the art of offering.

What is offered—says the late Barthes about Japan[3]—is far less important than the offering itself, than the wrapping. Decoration is the opposite of both orderlessness and imperative symmetry. High decorative art subtly installs the asymmetrical so as to generate movement. Barthes's *déplacement* completely fulfills this desire to generate movement while offering. Frontal, explicit, firm positing would immediately make the enchantment of offering evaporate into obligation. The higher art of decorative offering is precisely not about obliging the other. Barthes writes offeringly, not positingly.

The insight into the possibility of intellectual nonobligation is Barthes's main contribution.

Love obliges, infatuation does not. The former is a law, the latter is ruleless—or at least it promises rulelessness. Barthes's entire oeuvre is governed by an elegant mechanism of evasion. The work has many infatuations, few great loves. And, for that matter, only the first stages of infatuation: the figure in the distance, on the other side of the dance floor or the subway car. No glances have crossed, no first names have been exchanged, the infatuated has seen only a gesture, a detail that captures him like the photographic punctum. No reciprocity, no resistance whatsoever of information, of another biography. Barthes holds infatuation against love. This attitude explains the brilliant elegance of his work; a decorative sophistication that makes his entire work, every sentence, every theory read like a spiraling arabesque.

His fragmentary, noncommittal treatment of images seems above all a way of shielding his naked sensitivity to gesture. He finds those gestures in images, but at a distance, collectively, stripped of their obscene power by culture. In images, he escapes the body, which performs the gesture but thereby also makes it far too concrete—he does not look at bodies but at gestures in spite of the body. In writing, through images, he escapes the gripping corporeality of our existence. For Barthes, the gesture is like an image, against the body. In an image, the gesture once more doubles its distance.

The gesture is a reference point for Barthes. It happens in the body but infinitely transcends it; it speaks but without language, it is creative but without intended meaning, it is extremely visible and yet veiled, at once material and transcending all materiality, at once irresponsible and fatal. Gestures are fascinating because they are illegible and therefore as alienating as the gestures of an automaton. Gestures are empty signs to which the unconscious links phantasmatic scenarios. Gestures are empty and stand for something else: they are Barthes's ultimate fetish. In gesture, something is averted: both denied and indirectly addressed. In gesture, something is averted: proximity.

Images have power over the imagination. That is precisely why their control has always been so important. Barthes never showed patience toward that control by aesthetics (to summarize many instances in one word). Images are primordial instruments of power. Even more than architecture (too functional) or theater (too transient), the image is the ideal occupying force for the subject. No history of art can paper over this main theme of the visual arts. It immediately raises problems of responsibility: every image occupies me and appeals to me. The image is a princely privilege, turning me into a believer no matter what.

The democratic image does not change the natural sympathy between the image and power, between spectator and believer. There is just a lot of hypocrisy and denial. In aristocratic regimes, the image is the extension of an unquestionable genealogy. The image embodies that continuity. This immediately produces an uncomplicated relationship to tradition, which can be handled both more intensely and more loosely. In democratic regimes, tradition is subject to ontological doubt by democracy about its past and a questionable investment in its future. Market and fashion rather than genealogy.

Barthes wards off the democratic image by reducing it to text—that is, to structure. He wards off the image by taming it under the sign of communication and functionality into a rather banal instrument. He refuses to face the violence of the image—until it ends up revealing itself to him as the Medusa[4]: the photograph as Commendatore.[5]

His relationship to images is occasional, not fundamental. There is pleasure involved, but no responsibility. The images do not demand an explanation from him; he masticates them. It is a relationship of tasting, never a response to an appeal. For Barthes, images are without obligations whatsoever. He chooses them regardless of and even deliberately against the *surmoi de la culture* [the superego of culture] (François Wahl[6]). Images liberate something in him. They are the site of resistance to responsibility par excellence.

This happy relationship to images is a naive one, too. For him, images are vacation. Something vacant in their proximity is declared vacant. He advertises a vacancy: a call for words and ideas to fill the empty space of the images.

Images appear as unsuspecting savages in his universe. He massages and hugs them as *enfants sauvages* whom he teaches the word. Barthes as a shepherd in an arcadian iconology. His book on photography is in large part and against his better judgment the ultimate manifestation of that hypothesis: he works down a long list of infatuations, waiting for the last image that will cut him loose from all the others, like an obsessive shopper relieved to find that his bank card no longer works.

Except for that last image, no image holds a riddle up to Barthes. Images never force themselves upon him; they are noncommittal occasions. No *invisible* manifests itself through a fragile *visible*. No epiphany, no religiosity whatsoever (that flip side of the coin of the power in and of the image). For Barthes, every image is a banal projection surface, a mirror for the spectator, the ideological echo of a culture. Images, in short, the way publicity and propaganda like them. Barthes writes about images as if they can all be considered exclusively from the point of view of consumer society. Banal, perfect phantoms of the society of the spectacle.

Barthes's image selections are whimsical rather than truly surprising. He wrote about images at the request of others. Often the request is a first encounter. He looks without prior knowledge, that is, without acquaintance, without being interested in making acquaintance. The writing is a slow digestive process. Never superficial, but always a closed monologue.

He renounces what every art critic and historian of any ambition strives for because it is the prerequisite for his "right to speak," namely the forming of one's own taste. A taste that guides and motivates likes and dislikes, that makes distinctions that really matter to the critic. There is not the slightest trace of such a development in Barthes. His refinement has remarkably little to do with taste. I suspect him of being insensitive to taste. As a matter of principle, because taste rests on experience and supports authority.

His work lacks the pleasure of nuance, the colorful palette of judgments of taste. It is no accident that he disdains the adjective. It is no accident that he molds adjectives into rigid substantives by means of the suffix "-ité." The entire vocabulary of sensibility is thus publicly executed by Barthes. The substantive is the guillotine of taste—the latter is too corporeal and intimate.

Barthes is preeminently "modern." Not a combative and self-confident prewar-style modernist but self-evidently "modern," as everyone is from the 1950s onward, enraptured by the inexhaustible novelty generated by industrialized consumption. The self-evidently modern is what all of Tati's films are about. Not an ideological cultural project but obviousness. One must be modern because everyone is modern: tautology. Modernism, on the other hand, is preeminently a debate, which the moderns have replaced with inventory and description. Modernism was in the hands of artists; the modern is in the hands of academic exegetes who present themselves not as cultural experts but as social experts. Modernists swear by movements, the moderns embrace communication as a model and issue. Modernists embody marginal protest, the moderns manage renewal at the center of society. This is the difference between the 1920s and the 1950s.

Both—the modernists with their right convictions and the moderns with their right possessions—share the same foundational grammatical form: they make obsolete what came before. To be modern, they must declare something "no longer possible." The modern separates the *to do* from the *no longer done*. This is a repetitive castration of history. What lies beyond that law no longer has any value: what is obsolete is removed from stock. Completely. No nostalgic retrospection, no references to apprenticeship, no recognition of a legacy. So much liquidation makes one lonely and tempts one to take part in a modernist movement or a modern trend, in a military system or in a fashion. Where diachronic continuity expires, synchronous collections emerge.

Once the fashion has been promulgated, modern consumer society offers radical evenness: everything is juxtaposed with the same denominator of objectifying distance. Everything is reduced to its effectiveness, that is, measured by its success. Success on one horizontal level each time: that of economy, that of technology, that of communication, that of *signification*. Formal reduction to information, product, exchange value or Signifier. All geared toward social streamlining. The moderns provided both the analysis and the legitimization of this streamlining.

The Barthesian distance is an essential component of modern, fashionable streamlining; one does not step out of the system with it, but creates its condition. Because the moderns do not tolerate engagement (against the stream) and presuppose distance (no resistance, therefore, but streamlining).

What does Barthes—the ultimate incarnation of the moderns—put out of fashion? *No longer done*: subordination, syllogism, diachrony, dialectics, history, explanation, conclusion, morality. The symbolic sign par excellence is the disjunctive "/," not the concluding "=" or the "\." The slash is an opposition only in the first instance, because in the second instance that opposition is seen as an equivalence: not a dialectical opposition but two interchangeable positions on either side of a dividing line. A mathematical, not an existential figure. It is at once the fold on which all decorative arabesques rest. It does not open a discussion or exchange, but an enumeration: Barthes takes full part in the culture of lists, of inventorying *numérotage*. His central model is the catalog, his basic intellectual apparatus the category, his basic production neologisms, his core vocabulary prefixes and suffixes.

The slash also makes clear another obsession of the moderns: their fear of mixture and multiplication, their desire for separate classification and their predilection for reproduction. Language, once very rashly declared by Barthes to be fascist, is mixture, contamination, impurity par excellence. Words are fundamentally never new. Supposedly for scientific reasons but in fact for stylistic reasons, Barthes accomplished a gigantic expansion of the patrimony of the French language. After him, French became another language.

Barthes's criticism of petty-bourgeois myths, too, is mostly repugnance to their impurity. Moderns and modernists share the same existential disgust with mixing from which—incidentally—the nineteenth century drew its very strength. The purity of reflection and its expression are a twentieth-century obsession. The poverty of that purity becomes the main problem of the second Barthes, who seeks a pure way out of purity with *le plaisir*. For Barthes will always remain a Protestant *purificateur*. How could he have loved images? It is no accident that film is too sticky for him, too much bourgeois mythology. It is no accident that he writes very sophisticated texts about infatuation but hardly anything about eroticism.

Barthes rescues himself and us from purity time and again—from the cleanliness of modern design and ditto detergents—with his festive thinking. Unlike the somber, red-dominated colors of Bataille and Foucault, Barthes shines with an impressionistic palette applied to a white undercoat. His dominant color is rococo blue. Each text is a gift wrapped in joy and offered. His ideas don't want to be terror but conversation. Every sentence the perfect balance between maximum sharpness and maximum space for the reader. An intellectual life—unique in the twentieth century—imbued with one moral principle, that of the *délicatesse* in which distance and tenderness, the sharpness of the teacher and the caution of the host are balanced. What is missing is recklessness and the violence of eroticism. It is enough to read Pasolini and Barthes side by side to see the difference.

Anyway, I love the bourgeois side of Barthes. The supposed critic of bourgeoisness—in its consumer version—is obviously its best connoisseur but also its ultimate spokesman. From modernity he did not so much retain the seemingly critical potential (we already saw how the moderns embody and do not criticize the ideals of the new world) but above all an elegant, somewhat haughty self-aestheticization. The systematization by the semiologist and structuralist serves a tempered sensuality, not a hysterical identification with newness. In Barthes, the art of living for the benefit of consumer society prevails.

More than anybody else, Barthes distrusts the authority of cultural tradition. He does not draw authority from culture. He distrusts erudition. In doing so, he misses an important other figure: erudition as resistance, culture as a challenge, the complexity of the past as a task. Culture is a brilliant and indispensable means of arming oneself against fashion.

Barthes has always considered the authority of bourgeois culture as a process of naturalization: the created, contingent, historically grown culture transformed into a once-and-for-all natural self-evidence. But instead of addressing the historical process itself, he examines its caricatural reduction into a myth. This is clever, but it is also evasion: he is not part of a tradition; he does not set himself against it. He describes the lie of the modern myth and considers the mechanics of that myth to be the only truth to be discovered and gained. It is as if only the myth exists, as if only the phantasmagoria of the society of the spectacle is real—in its very mythic status. Only the unreal is real. For Debord, it is an ontological scandal of the first order, but Barthes embraces it so as to escape an even more terrifying illusion: that of an alternative truth, that of an "obligation."

Barthes ultimately briefly accepts one law, as imperative and arbitrary as the language sign, namely the system of structures. The structure of the list and the alphabet, the structure of a geometrical deduction, the system of free-floating equivalences. An empty system that doesn't operate through external reference but through internal coherence. An empty system as the rules of a game. Without content, it allows for endless playing. The transcendence of the rules of the game over any game and all possible players is at once a decorative but undoubtedly also a subliminally erotic dream. Against the compelling coherence of the rules, the radical interchangeability of the players. Barthes's ambition is to coincide with the empty place of the abstract player from the rules and thus to withdraw from the overfull space in the game that is played.

For Barthes does not want to be addressed, not even as a player. In language, he is a distant "him," an aloof "Roland Barthes," as Simenon writes of Monsieur Bouvet,[7] as the janitor speaks of her tenants, as Jupien speaks of M. de Charlus.[8] Especially in language, one does not pat Barthes on the back—just as, according to Truffaut, one could not pat Hitchcock on the back either.[9]

Barthes doesn't have any secrets, but he hates confidences and gossip. Interpretative explanations are of the same order, whether social, psychological or aesthetic. No causality, no motivation, no underlying secrets, no detective work. That means no layering, no dialectics of appearance and truth, but pure functioning. No more mediations by interpretations, but the immediacy of the system. Pure form, the zero degree of description that says what is there as clearly as a mirror, without suggesting any surplus. We are in a sophisticated fetishistic brothel, in which the system functions like a liturgy. Precisely where there is nothing (nothing but what is), ritual is crucial.

It is certainly no accident that Barthes—the asexual seducer—enchanted a generation that remained entangled in insoluble oedipal conflicts. No accident that Barthes used the word "fascist" when he condemned language. In doing so, he activated the trauma of all his listeners who knew perfectly well what was at stake in such a catastrophic condemnation. An oedipal conflict that in those sentences acquired ontological radicality. Not by contemplating history but precisely by turning it into a myth.

Barthes perfectly illustrates the impasse of aestheticized intellectuality: when things are only form and are no longer heard as an appeal, are not taken up as responsibility.

This way, Barthes seems like the main character of a decadent novel, ending in the obsessive *face à face* with an image, of all things. An image that confronts him with irreducible reality: absence. A terrifying revolution—no more tilting of the modern conviction that all is the sum of what is present here and now in the synchronous system of actuality. What is not present, because it is inactual, does not exist. That is the condition for modern society's celebration, of which Barthes more than anybody else sang the praises, which he made self-conscious, but of which he never showed us the emergency exit.

Portrait of a Role: the Intellectual[1]

The intellectual is a role. It is not a specific talent, trait or IQ; nor is it a specific social function: there is no training for it, no statute, no professional profile. That is why "role" seems to be the best term. Society declares this "role" vacant for those who have the calling. "Intellectual" is not a characteristic of an individual but a relationship—with other roles and therefore with objects of value to which all roles have to relate. One can take on the role but also retire from it. One can take it on briefly, intermittently, or for a long time. It is a vacant place.

What is the definition of this role? What elements, or perhaps more accurately, what tensions define the role? Of what forces is the intellectual the intersection? How can a concrete individual take on that role and give it its own identity? To what tendencies is the role exposed? What traps are implicit in it? What is its inherent limitation? These have been the questions I started asking myself while writing. Sometimes it was helpful to refer to other roles, such as the amateur and the critic, in order to clarify the characteristics I wanted to emphasize.

1.

Being an intellectual is not a profession. The intellectual has a profession, for example professor of philosophy, but manifests himself as an intellectual only when he operates outside his profession, when he ventures outside his competence. Hence the slightly provocative, but perhaps not entirely incorrect idea that the intellectual is by definition "nonprofessional," as he makes his appearance when his professional competence ends. Taking on the role of an intellectual therefore implies that he becomes an equal of his fellow citizens and puts the head start of his profession between brackets. Because he makes statements that go beyond his professional sphere, because he passes value judgments within his professional sphere without being able to justify those value judgments from his professional competence. The intellectual role provides the professional with the opportunity to think "freely," relieved of methodological discipline. In other words, the role of the intellectual allows people and thoughts to meet in a nonspecialized, nonprofessionalized sphere. That intellectuals do not know what they are talking about is, in a sense, always a pertinent remark. It is the intellectual's task (and privilege) to venture outside the work sphere. Within the specialized work sphere, one is (for many reasons, by the way) no longer able to approach things "with an open mind." This open-mindedness could easily be branded as naivety.[2] Naive are all those who do not conform to the limits of professionalism and wish to maintain freedom of judgment on other, human grounds. Of course, the fear of being reproached with unprofessionalism is as strong today as the fear of not being authorized and of thinking on one's own was before. The intellectual is the one who does not hide behind the authority of a profession and asks naive questions. Not all naive questions are intellectual questions; in the case of the intellectual, it involves a combative, committed naivety (but is that still a correct use of the word?).

2.

The intellectual is the one who assumes responsibility, who "under oath" gives his view of the facts, of the problem. He is the one who effectively hears and answers the question, "What is your idea, belief, reaction?" In fact, each of us is constantly asked that question; it is the most crucial social question there is. The question is also constantly begged. Social cynicism is an effective way of dismissing that question as an archaeological phantasm—of not hearing it.

Hearing the social question is one thing, answering it another. The role of the intellectual seems to lie primarily in that answer, but I think his answer is especially important because he is able to let the question shine through. His answer is secondary, although the answer is often used to stifle the question once again. So that's what the intellectual is for, for raising the matter of justification, for recalling society's implicit question about everyone's position.

Of course, the one (the aforementioned noncompetence) has everything to do with the other (responsibility). Indeed, responsibility is not acquired through competence. The question is not posed only to those who are competent, but to everyone. Competence gives more body to responsibility, but it does not create it. Responsibility—as a repercussion of the question that rises from the social body—considers all citizens of equal moral capital. A capital, besides, that every citizen manages on behalf of everyone else. The social question is also always one of cocitizenship: how would I act in your place, how would you act in mine? Would you want to adopt their behavior? Would you want others to utter your answer? The questions the intellectual hears are questions about living and acting together.

That is why the interventions of the intellectual are his own and therefore personal opinions which do not, however, express the idiosyncratically individual (as is the task of the critic) but immediately become fundamental positions against other positions.[3] However extreme Pasolini's polemical positions in the last years of his life, they could never be neutralized as poetic freedom but were always responsible social acts. The intellectual manifests himself with his opinion in a social field, the critic, on the other hand, primarily in the realm of private sensibility which cannot, in the final analysis, be contested or argued. The critic must be excitingly unpredictable. The critic speaks on his own behalf; so does the intellectual but among and against others. The critic starts from an inner impulse, the intellectual from an impulse outside himself. The critic does not answer the fundamental social question but is given the chance to play the game of unjustified judgment.

Curiously, being a critic is a "profession" nonetheless—one can train as a critic, and there are professional associations and social structures of recognition.[4] There is also a clear professional competence of the critic: developed and informed personal taste. Nothing similar exists for the intellectual.

3.

Knowledge feeds judgment but it does not generate it; familiarity with a case sustains a decision but it does not determine it. Judging and acting are of a different order than knowing and investigating. Whoever acts, has to deal with the resistance of facts and means—a crucial kind of resistance is the fact that whoever acts, changes the situation that seemed to compel that action, so that the intended effects can never be achieved. To act is to set a situation in motion and thus to carry out that action in a different situation. Something similar also happens to judgment, which one irrevocably passes as a person. One "knows" in an impersonal, shared way, but one always judges personally.[5] This clouds judgment, making it impure, irrelevant, unobjective, but also eminently human.

The question, of course, is whether and how knowledge can nurture and inspire action and judgment. Can the intellectual at the end of the day do something with knowledge and information? The question is grotesque—"of course," you tend to think. Without knowledge you cannot take responsibility but, on the other hand, knowledge does not make the responsibility any lighter. Knowledge does not act and does not judge. It is in itself an amorphous, available, dead object. Indeed, only action and judgment elevate knowledge into living social and moral substance.

This inadequacy of knowledge does not delight me, quite on the contrary. The private and fatal nature of acting and judging flatters my vanity only briefly—immediately afterward it becomes a source of shudders and awe at its mythical proportions.

4.

The intellectual does not simply work in the media—he is the product of it. He is inconceivable outside the media: his role only exists on that podium, in that play. The stage on which he is standing the Germans call *Feuilleton*. The media—a phenomenon dating from the eighteenth century—is a social system outside of which the intellectual cannot exist.

An immediate consequence is that the intellectual addresses an anonymous audience. This anonymity induces a number of rhetorical poses that determine the language, but especially the content, way of thinking, and self-image.

Even before the intellectual appeared on the stage, there was—of course—thought, writing, and discussion about the themes that the intellectual ordinarily tackles: the state of society, the actions of fellow citizens, the task of the state, the limits of its power. But this was done in a different configuration—more intimate, more concentrated, more sustained.

The intellectual reflects on the rhythm of the media, that is, on the pulse of current events. His thinking is not guided by the everyday but by the exceptional incident. His thinking is not a "strolling contemplation," but is controlled by the economic necessity of the media to make a difference every day. "Checking off" is the fundamental style—but fatally also the intellectual's fundamental way of thinking. Sharpness, elegance, and economy are the intellectual's great intellectual-literary qualities. This endangers true intellectual labor, which is the inner conquest of an object and of the object's own thinking rather than a quick reply. Speed is the modern quality par excellence.

The older society was oriented toward reputation and example. These are two slow principles, far removed from the risks of current events and the whims of opinion. Both—reputation and example—constitute a symbolic capital which a society hands out as a compass, as an immediate conversion machine for judging and acting. Reputation and example do not apply to exemplary persons but to the functioning of exemplarity; society does not need truly exemplary people but it does need the example as symbolic currency.[6]

In the media system—a system of topicality—no reputation is safe. In the system of the anonymous mass of the media, abstract exemplarity does not suffice; every example must be fitted with extreme concreteness.[7] It takes a body, a unique smile, the uniqueness of sexuality to construct the modern example. The modern example is therefore anything but exemplary. It is all too human, while the exemplary is obviously inhuman.

After the erosion and decay of reputation and exemplum, society lacks a handy compass, a quick conversion table. The intellectual has taken that place—changing it thoroughly, of course, so that it is no longer the same place. The intellectual is a real-time converter of topical matters.

5.

Whoever writes about the intellectual is, of course, themself an intellectual. The role is autoproclamative. This results in a strange structure: the role of the intellectual is immune to external criticism—not because it is indifferent to it but because no function for external criticism exists. No one has written out the intellectual's task and is able to evaluate its performance (the teacher, however, is). Just as a conscience cannot be commented upon by any other authority, imposing itself as compelling obviousness with which any discussion is in vain, so it goes with the intellectual.

He is fully immersed in society but finds himself at the same time in a metaposition above and beyond the social. That metaposition can no longer be subjected to external judgment. A sociology of the intellectual aims at candidates but not at the role itself. As soon as it is brought up, one is inside the intellectual argument and the intellectual role. The role supplies its self-criticism and self-justification.

The intellectual role does not lose any sleep over this: it considers itself eminently self-critical. But the role's untouchability remains and raises questions. The extreme critical sense does not change that moment of uncriticizability. That he is a servant of a social logic mitigates the individual circumstance of who is playing the role at that moment, not the underlying principle. The intellectual therefore occupies a kind of king's place within a democracy. Without investiture—as befits a democracy. There is no constitution, there are no professional rules—after all, the intellectual's being an intellectual is not a profession. The intellectual operates according to an unspoken logic. It is an essential task of the intellectual constantly to name, test, and question that logic. The intellectual constantly asks the question of legitimacy (especially of his own function). This adds a fair dose of narcissism to the autoproclamativity.

6.

The intellectual is always an intellectual of and for the present. He fits into the industrial culture that invests exclusively in that present. The present is the fraction within which one can intervene in the course of things: to make profits, to take power, to exert influence. The present is like a ball in the game: one can score a goal only when one has the ball.

The present is the game of chance we are all hooked to, ensnared in. Even the venerable art of investing has fallen under this regime. The intellectual role is certainly not cut out for criticizing and parrying that. Only if one renounces that role can one begin to stand a chance of breaking through the passion of the present.[8]

The twentieth-century intellectual has considered it his duty to thematize the present object but also to intervene in the present tense. A utopian kind of immediacy (in my own vocabulary this is called "experience") is pursued—and a utopian closeness to fellow citizens, contemporaries, fellow spectators, fellow consumers. The intellectual constantly speaks "on behalf" of others—actually, they are precisely not others but like-minded people. Despite evidence to the contrary, the intellectual is a very socially alert creature, concentrated on others' opinions. He thinks on his own, it seems, yet constantly with an eye toward others as beacons for his course. The intellectual is the situated intellect par excellence—situated in a body and its preferences, in a biography and its experiences, in topicality and what it has to offer.

Immediacy is all that remains when the transcendent has become unthinkable, morality private, and society amoral. Into this stifling immediacy, the intellectual today squeezes a tool —psychology, sociology, theories of meaning—so as to give volume to it. Immediacy is one-dimensional, and the intellectual wants to cut it some slack, give it depth. This leads to an ironic version of the intellectual, whereas the intellectual role was once played very pathetically. A role that was once borne by the indignation that we have every reason to still feel today but no longer seem to have the arguments or the temperament for.[9] The intellectual today is as situated as ever, but hardly committed anymore. The present is no longer the fraction within which one thinks one can put a "no" to the world; at the very most it is about tearing off its—very last—clothes. The present is no longer the fraction within which one thinks one can change the course of the game but at most the fraction within which one scores a goal. The intellectual is a hunter, no longer a reformer. He hunts illusions—especially those of reformers.[10] But he no longer reaches out, no longer suggests a direction, no longer points to what is obviously no longer possible and what obviously must be.[11] No reform, however, without the passion of intellectuals—without that passion, reform is just everyday opportunism.

7.

The intellectual has a dubious, problematic relationship to acting, to action. He is fundamentally the nonactor, the one who weighs action, at most steers it but does not lead it. Nor is he the philosopher alongside the prince but rather the voice from the chorus, the commentary in the margin. The intellectual can enter politics but then he is no longer an intellectual. The function does not allow the touch of doing.

After all, the intellectual is supposed to be independent. An ironic demand, of course, if we have been situating him in the media right from the start. The intellectual is not an aristocratic amateur but, on the contrary, the intellect that must at the same time sell itself on the market of opinions and defend, if not reality, at least the semblance of autonomy. But precisely this ambiguity makes him ideally suited to understand certain movements, positions, maneuvers in society. His independence is never de facto but always to be gained. He is a worker who experiences, articulates and evaluates the contradictions of the service.

He is therefore a questionable figure—without legitimation for his authority, without authority since he eschews action and never needs to put things to the test.

8.

The intellectual is diametrically opposed to the amateur. The intellectual often allows himself to be seduced into authority and by authority, something the amateur has no propensity for. The intellectual's independence is constantly embedded in a political definition of it (freedom of opinion, for example). What's more, he derives much of his authority from the social relevance of his discussion, which ultimately must also be stated in political terms. Politicians borrow arguments from intellectuals. After he has answered the big question, there is always a "what should we do next?" Although the intellectual is not the prince's philosopher, he constantly speaks the language of political responsibility. He has a hard time resisting the dubious charms of that kind of responsibility.

The amateur is an entirely different story. He does not think in terms of educating others but of generous curiosity. He is curious about the combination of his being and the world, of his preferences and what the world has to offer. The surprises that occur in the touching of these two "systems" are the amateur's subject. For him, every experience is a basis for radical irresponsibility. The curiosity of the amateur for impression is fundamentally unlimited. He is not looking for the object that would satisfy his desire and close his curiosity—that closure is impossible.

Very differently fares the intellectual who constantly reasons in terms of completion, of a potential point of harmony, of a projectable point of equilibrium. The amateur does not think in terms of equilibrium but of unlimited accumulation of experiences.

The amateur is a nontopical role. His disposition discredits him, while it used to be the very basis of expertise. The curiosity of the amateur is a source of caution and endless nuances—which today are misunderstood as a lack of clear insight, organization, and consistency. The amateur thinks—but without metathought, without a method, without epistemological obsession. His thinking derives its particularity precisely from the absence of an objectifiable method.

When the amateur manifests himself, he does so in an aristocratic register: sparing, reserved, for insiders. The knowledge of the amateur is of a kind that unfortunately no longer has a place today. It is a variant of *le discours amoureux*, whose radical nontopicality was demonstrated by Barthes. Nevertheless, the curious egoism of the amateur has a more important social role than one might suspect. He is the one who shows that the fanaticism of his obsessional "care" is so much richer than that of the curator-as-janitor who wants to make his premises—abandoned by the ruined legitimate occupants—inexorably profitable. The amateur dwells, and that is the ultimate luxury. The intellectual does not dwell; his sense of urgency has something irrevocably vulgar. The intellectual is never aristocratic.

9.

The intellectual is not an *être de connaissance* but an *être de jugement*.[12] Taking sides, and making take sides, is his job. That is, he does not reason in terms of "and-and" but of "or-or." His style is exclusive, not inclusive. He chooses caricature to clarify the polarity. His rhetoric tends toward polarization and exaggeration. This is a formidable rhetorical strategy that produces a special kind of knowledge: opinion. The nature of opinion is not nuance but demarcated opposition. Polemic and catastrophism are the basic genres of his style.

Yet precisely choosing knowledge-as-judgment (rather than knowledge-as-fact) is of immense significance. Life impels tough decisions, effective choices (between yes and no, between doing and doing nothing). The entire register of life that must be lived without nuance (isn't that the most frightening and exalting thing about life?) is expressed by knowledge as polar judgment rather than by knowledge as a nuanced presentation of facts.

The intellectual role is fundamentally vitalistic; the intellectual cultivates urge-based thinking. This urge is easily expressed in the fundamental rhetorical structure of his thinking, namely polemical polarity. The intellectual "inverts" (sees the backside, ironizes, ignores). Cynicism is always within reach. The intellectual problematizes "as a matter of principle" because the truth for him always lies on the other side of the so-called self-evident reality. The cynical inversion is his heuristic principle. Yet the cynical intellectual is an impossibility: he would become a politician or a ghostwriter. The cynic no longer has any "own" ideas, only the negation of all other ideas. The intellectual employs the cynical principle as an instrument of thought, but cynicism as an attitude is fatal to his role. (Difference between adjective and substantive—would it be that simple? Isn't such an elegant reduction to a grammatical contrast cynical?)

The intellectual is a systematic punisher of *mauvaise foi* [bad faith]. But if there is anyone fundamentally ill-willed—and proud of it too— it is the intellectual who is driven not by understanding but by judging, not by complexity but by the simplicity of an antagonistic figure. In this sense, then, the intellectual is not a "sage." The latter is looking for balanced self-evidence, for serene versatility. The intellectual replies to every so-called self-evidence with the excavation of its background, with the merciless revelation of its archeology. The sage cultivates putting things into perspective, the intellectual cultivates indictment: he is the examining magistrate who regards every essence as an attack on his perspicacity; he is the tax inspector who regards every wisdom as an attempt to escape the toll of thinking. The "sage" leaves distrust for what it is; the intellectual declares distrust to be an essential instrument of knowledge.

The instruments of the intellectual today certainly serve desolidarization and the abolishing of membership. Here, we see the intellectual's bounds exceeded. His role seems to have become a systematic demolition of connections. At that point, he is ready to become a party ideologue, the ultimate betrayal of the intellectual role.

10.

The intellectual has a task—so he always proudly says and thinks of himself. He is a peculiar cousin in the great family of civil servants and liberal professions that so explicitly carried out a social mission in the last century.

The intellectual calls for responsibility: at once a demand for an answer and a demand to act accordingly. "Surely we can no longer…" This dialogical game is at the basis of the intellectual's intense awareness of the interwovenness of actions and statements. (In cynicism, precisely that interwovenness is dissolved.) The intellectual role rests on knowing that coexistence, thought, morality, and culture exist as a weave that holds everyone together and connects everyone to the past. The intellectual exists only through the hypothesis that what is said and especially what is not said, what is thought and especially what is not thought, what is done and especially what is not done has consequences. This is the pole of continuity that underpins the intellectual role. It contrasts sharply with that other pole already described, in which the intellectual preeminently represents the principle of polarization, adhering to a systematic undermining of continuity as a result of which his dialogue always manifests itself as contradiction. The intellectual's great conservative impulse (wanting to preserve the weave) is threatened precisely by the cutting, discontinuous instrument he wields.

Whoever bears responsibility, has attention. Responsibility is not a moody reflex, not a capricious "yes or no," but a process that presupposes pondering over and weighing the pros and cons. Weighing is only possible in a climate of attention. Attention to two opposites. On the one hand, attention to memory, to temporal continuity, to developments and evolutions. But another kind of attention is necessary too, that of the incommensurability of every occurrence (of a situation, action, utterance, idea, piece of work). Attention to the unrepeatable, to the uniquely particular. Attention to continuity automatically generalizes, recognizing rules and structures, stability in change. The intellectual is confronted with the problems of all practitioners: doctors, lawyers, educators, therapists, priests, artists. They know so well that each instance stands alone, that each instance is *the* exception to the known rule.

The intellectual's attention is therefore torn: between the weave (which provides stability, also in his thinking) and uniqueness (which inevitably provides instability and unreasonableness, and often provides the intellectual with very beautiful moments). "The instance" is by definition unreasonable, *hors raison*. The unique instance can not be known, only assessed. One can never say of the unique what it is, only what its effect is.

Responsible attention is thinking together, alongside. It is not thinking in someone else's place but in exchange with them. "What would I (think, do, feel) in their place?" Responsibility is daring to recognize the other place. But you can see how that "thinking together" can become "positing by proxy." The intellectual then becomes a partisan (partisanship is the metamorphosis of the other into "one's own party"). The intellectual role excludes partisanship, while it does constantly take sides, in the sense of "taking someone's side," "walking alongside someone."

Those who find the nuance between partisanship and solidarity too sophisticated, choose haughty, bitter irresponsibility.[13] How could one ever stand and think together with the other? Of all places, the place of the other must be respected as radically unknowable. Of all things, one must resist the temptation of the other's place. An imaginary place for illusory identifications. The intellectual role excludes this epistemological and cultural relativism. The weave allows seeing particularity and participating in it.

11.

The intellectual is a writer. From this follows a way of acting while thinking: no exposition, no argumentation, no logical method, exasperatingly implicit self-evidences that are not up for discussion. What's more, in his writing the aleatory plays an important role—the aleatory that characterizes everyday life. In that impure space, insights are not put into practice, conclusions are overlooked, predictable consequences irrationally ignored. The intellectual thinks impulsively and thus often inconsistently, according to his temperament. In the face of new information and insights, habit offers beneficial and sometimes catastrophic resistance. Flaws? Of course, but perhaps also a great quality that only he can manifest within responsibility.

Either way, a systematic intellectual with a logical system shifts away from the intellectual role. His logic is always playful, his argumentation always a caricature, his arguments often one-sided. Yet he is concerned with something else; he must do justice to the complexity of the subject, to the elusive capriciousness and complexity of his own reactions to it.

The intellectual is an occasional thinker and writer. His form is the brief, time-bound intervention. A book doesn't suit him—his book is at most a collection of "flying sheets."[14] The intellectual is local and momentary. He is a practice-bound thinker; he is also a practical think-er. He wants to do something by thinking. He belongs to the family of the caricaturist, the cartoonist. He shares the fact that he too wants to strike (be striking and offensive).

The intellectual as a writer uses language as a source for thinking, not as a means of thinking. He lets language think for him. For him, language is an active aid, not a passive medium. Hence the fact that there is a deep incommensurability between the intellectual and language on the one hand and the media and their standardized language on the other. Language in the media is a channel for facts—a reduction of opinions to demagogic polls. Imagery gives facts a symbolic dimension—a game that cannot be played in the media. (Advertising and slogans employ functional imagery, a one-dimensional game that deprives imagery of its uncontrollable freedom.)

The furthest the media want to go with language is wordplay, which never shows a love of language, let alone a love of thought. No, the lan-guage of the intellectual is not mediagenic. Language must be able to get the better of the intellectual so as to see where the vehicle called "language" can take thinking, his thinking. At the same time, he must constantly discipline, purify, and reprimand language; he must chide the hysteria and euphoria of his language in order never to lose touch with the brutality of the language of collectivity.

For one of the intellectual's tasks is to speak in a language without specialization. Two tendencies threaten that project today. On the one hand, intelligible language is equated with mediatized, instrumental-ized language. A language stripped of its imaginary potentiality, of its layeredness, of its ambiguity. On the other hand, there is the methodo-logical project for the "scientific" humanities—a crucial condition for this is the artificial metalanguage in which neologisms must univocally indicate a concept, a procedure. A technical code, a military command language, a traffic code that is erroneously presented as the primal form of language. This artificial language projects its own structure onto its subject of research and declares natural language to be a code, too. This has often proved irresistible for the intellectual role—sterile metalanguage, the hypothesis of the code promised modernist purity. But the fascination that this solution exerts, is fatal to the intellectual role: the latter is fundamentally impure.

Sociology and semiology tilted the intellectual function. These disciplines proposed a level of description and inquiry to the researcher that is no longer observable but can only be evoked within the categories of the inquiry. This is an order *hors expérience* and therefore *hors responsabilité*. A level that is devalued, demoralized, where assessment is no longer possible. This is the copernican revolution of the humanities— the installation of a level that can be observed but no longer politicized.[15] Postmodernity draws the consequence of hypermoralism from this impossibility—the impossibility to grasp the objects of late-modern research still in a moral, political, that is to say active and responsible way.

The intellectual—of politics, of art—has become an intellectual of culture. Not a critic of morals but an observer of the code. Why not a critic of the code? Precisely because the code escapes conscious responsibility in unlocalizable sociality.

Yet this legacy, including the culture of metalanguage, belongs to our time. The pose of metalanguage does not necessarily produce science, but it has become part of the artificial equipment of thinking—just as cars and airplanes have produced artificial but ubiquitous articulations of our space. A similar difficulty is at work in the place of scientific insight and information in the game of the intellectual role. Anyway: metalanguage does not make an intellectual, quite on the contrary.

12.

The realm of the intellectual is not objectivity, not the facts, not the law of what exists, but opinion, more specifically the thinking that guides and permeates life with desires and values and thus makes it worth living. The intellectual asks the question of value and of the conviction of that value. Opinion is not just dubious doxa but a shared inner appreciation that makes facts human, incorporates them into human history.

Not information but judgment is the intellectual's realm of activity. Of course judgment must be informed, but no matter how vast the mass of information, it never produces judgment. There is no *generatio spontanea* of judgment. Judgment never comes from the object, always from the I, here and now. Judgment is always situated, never objectified.

So the intellectual is not a scientist whose concern it is to think free from value judgments, to take an anonymous, repeatable position, to render the facts filtered of any value. Science presents us with the impossible ideal of objectivity—an objectivity that exists only between objects and becomes impossible as soon as a subject is involved. Science describes, the intellectual chooses, prefers one over the other, one against the other. That choice cannot be "proved"—you make a choice, you don't prove it. If you want to convince someone of the value of your choice, you have to come up with rhetorics, not with information. That rhetorical being is the intellectual.

His preference cannot be based on reasoning, debatable premises, and verifiable conclusions. This produces the typical idiosyncratic nature of the intellectual function that people often find offensive rather than an invitation to adventure.

13.

The intellectual is an extremely bourgeois figure. Together with his readers, he believes in improvability—that is, he is fundamentally modern. Where that belief is lacking, the moralist is at work, in a postmodern garb if need be. The latter brings disillusionment. He unmasks false pretensions. The intellectual, on the other hand, names the ideal.

The moralist names the immutable essence of humankind (a fallen being); the intellectual sees the possibility of humankind (humankind as a project). The media lack the long view of both the essence and the project. The media "believe" in nothing, neither in the unchanging anger and stupidity of human beings, nor in the improvability of their destiny. The "short view" of the media has become the short view of the whole contemporary world, where only pragmatism remains (that American project). Neither the cult of "what is," nor that of "what must be," but that of "what works." "What works" must be tested and invented again and again. Hence the aridity of contemporary egoism.

14.

It says a lot that the question of the intellectual today is being posed in an art magazine. It is a sign of the times that art commentary has become a refuge (or a testing ground?) for talking about morality, politics, the state of culture and thought today. Of course, the growing confusion between art and media facilitate this. Of course there is a megalomania in art about its social role as a ritual contestation of the existing order. Art is constantly puffed up by half-baked political theory. In the process, art's irresistible tendency to collaborate with the existing order is overlooked.

Commentary on art—an eighteenth-century creation as well—is something quite different from commentary on society, which is the role of the intellectual. Art commentary is rightly formulated from sensual pleasure and political opportunism. The childish selfishness of art is fundamental. The art critic shares in it. How many sensualists could design a full-fledged aesthetic politics from it? Diderot? Ruskin?

Even though art has much to do with power, it has never exercised power, not even today. If art has much to do with power, it is because great art supports power and bad art usually criticizes it. The task of the intellectual is essentially other than that of art. Art holds a natural claim—naive and scandalous, but repeatedly confirmed in practice—on a social state of exception.

The image celebrates what exists. The word problematizes it. The intellectual tends to iconoclasm—he (rightly) fears the immoral image. The critic at best shows off intellectualism and usually sears his wings on it; in fact, he shares the irresponsibility of art. How strange that power uses precisely that irresponsible, sensual (i.e., shrouded in passivity) image as its mirror.

In fact, the intellectual and the critic are in a fundamentally antinomic relation. The critic always comes after the facts; his task is to judge existing artworks, not to regulate the art to be made. He comes fundamentally and hopelessly (no, joyfully) after the facts, on principle embracing every appearance. After all, he asks for one thing only, more specifically for the next work, which should also preferably be "new," novel. Curiosity is the critic's basic passion; in principle, he is the most perfect media figure. The intellectual, on the other hand, distrusts novelty—it is always there too soon, too rash, too reckless, too irresponsible. The intellectual is fundamentally a conservative figure; calling the critic progressive for this reason, however, does not suit this purely moment-oriented sensualist.

The Sovereign Dandy[1]

Dress is the place of appearance, of illusion, of seduction. Dress is the main way for humankind to fit into the world, namely from behind a dividing line, a second skin. This double break between oneself and the world, as well as between oneself and one's own body, is the springboard for oneself-as-image. Dress is neither functional nor even real but ultimately purely imaginary: through dress one constructs an imaginary body for oneself.

Every morning everyone has to give form to that imaginary body. It is a very conscious ritual for women and appears to happen neutrally to men. Appearing neutral is a crucial aspect of a man's imaginary body image. For, of course, no one escapes the field of tension created by dress: neither the uniformed prison guard, nor the surgeon in green, nor the monk in his habit. They, too, irrevocably create that imaginary body, which simultaneously conceals and makes so much visible through that very concealment, albeit in another field, according to a different key.

Dressed for Authority

Those who aspire to authority (in a democracy) know that dress is crucial. In a subtle way, it must support that prestige, but not in such a way that it might seem that the dress created the very prestige. To be visible and yet not be seen, that is its mission.

The Dandy—a nineteenth-century figure—pursues moral authority, not effective power. He realizes that dress is of utmost importance in acquiring, maintaining, and making clear that moral authority. His dress must modulate the nature of that moral authority. Take, for instance, the great opponent of the Dandy, the bohemian. He too possesses considerable prestige—romantic and sentimental: one feels like taking care of him, one is endeared by the picturesque, the boyish lankiness, the robust *sans gêne* of old age. Everyone knows images of artists who have lived and dressed like this. But the Dandy stays away from that modality of prestige. Literally: keeping a distance is his mode of existence as well as his raison d'être.

This is a somewhat bizarre strategy, because in our type of society authority is focused on rapprochement, accessibility, seduction rather than impressing. Authority does not want to parade around naked but to pretend that it "doesn't mean it like that." The Dandy does mean it like that: he keeps a distance, strictly, imposingly, not to say provocatively. Not only through words and attitude, but also through dress he reprimands, bites back. Even those who are impressed should not think they can come into his favor or abide in his surroundings.

The Dandy is not a matter of fabric, cut, and attribute. It is a matter of attitude and expression. It is not enough to see the suit of a Dandy on a wooden mannequin to understand what is going on here. One has to imagine that attitude, that moral force, that cold energy along with it. Dress supports, but the living body directs. The Dandy is not a sartorial but a moral program (that is why I write the word with a capital letter). Hence the fact that you cannot exhibit him; each visitor must reconstruct the imaginary body of the Dandy within himself.

The Walking Stick

The Dandy is a character from the last century. Only a few specimens existed, and only in England and France—in London and Paris, to be exact. Yet they made a great impression; many pages have been devoted to their mystery. Described as heroic stylites, as exemplary lives. They are like young heroes of a feudal epic—only, they are living in the modern world, under the tyranny of science, democracy, and industry, that is, in a world without epic, with only novelistic possibilities. Hence some major differences: while the epic hero is pure and clear, the Dandy is characterized by ambiguity. The Dandy does not wield a sword but a walking stick; he does not wear a helmet but a top hat; he is not standing on a battlefield but in a park during a promenade concert, elegantly dodging horse poop on the sidewalk. His heroics have to do with social not bodily risks; not sword skills but quick-wittedness in a situation is crucial.

Three Phases

The Dandy evolves. This makes it hard to define him. He ends up in extravagant colors and eccentric behavior at the end of the century. He thus breaks the essential convention of restraint and understatement. He started out in London as a society phenomenon, as man's invention of fashion. But fashion is a matter both of dress and behavior. Dress is a social relation. Dandyism is its conscious cultivation. Between the London start and the fin de siècle decline, the crucial intellectual episode is two French texts by two French Dandies. Two sophisticated style exercises, showing unprecedented intellectual virtuosity. Dandyism becomes a manifesto of antiromanticism. They do not pursue expression and nature but artificiality; they do not know faith in universal good will, relying exclusively on distrustful self-defense. In texts by Barbey d'Aurevilly and Charles Baudelaire, the imaginary body image of the Dandy becomes a full-scale life project, in which dress is the externalization of a politics and ethics.

Impertinent

The Dandy is engaged in a competition; the relationship with fellow humans is polemical, challenging, provocative. The Dandy fits like a glove into the social struggle that will henceforth be waged ruthlessly—but without bloodshed—under the name of snobbery. With the crucial difference from banal snobbery being that the Dandy manages to be at once in the game and above it. After all, snobbery is "downward" disdain, temporary recognition of equals, and "upward" admiration. The Dandy never admires or acknowledges any one, he disdains. He is willing to pay any price for this position: he seeks radical solitariness He has no equals, for he is incomparable. He incarnates the principle of excellence, of the exceptional—through vigorous resistance to the democratic equality that no longer makes a difference. He does not have a "neighbor"—the Dandy is not a Christian character.

A Few Alternatives

To precisely recognize the strategy of the Dandy, it is necessary to position him correctly against related figures. The bohemian has already been mentioned. He is also an outsider, but too emphatically and therefore vulgarly antibourgeois. The Dandy stands for sophisticated detachment. Is he just an ordinary elegant man, as drawn by René Gruau in this century? Is he a lion, a macaroni as they were called in the beginning of the last century? Of course the Dandy is elegant, but his elegance is not to seduce but to deter: his elegance is glazed, icy, and unnatural. Everyone knows that elegance is inseparable from an impression of naturalness, of spontaneity: well, the Dandy is a protest against naturalness, he rejects any spontaneity. His seduction is not charming, but deadly, for the Dandy himself is never seduced. So his elegance is a trap, a promise that will most certainly not be kept.

In addition to the *bohémien* and the *élégant*, there is a role for the eccentric—especially in London. Of course the Dandy is eccentric, but he rejects the emphatic nature of the eccentric strategy. The Dandy is never extreme at first sight—on the contrary, he does not stand out naturally and immediately. Extravagance is an extreme, "wild," and therefore vulgar strategy, and the Dandy prefers to operate in an orderly fashion. What bothers most about the eccentric is that it addresses everyone arbitrarily, as unselectively as *réclame* [advertising]. The Dandy chooses by whom he wants to be noticed: he does not advertise.

Conservative

The Dandy is a conservative figure. In his study of Baudelaire, Jean-Paul Sartre rightly notes that Baudelaire's Dandyism was a protest without danger and consequence. But that is only half the story. After all, the Dandy obeys inner coherence not social effectiveness: he does not want to achieve anything, nor to change anything. Aren't there already enough messages of salvation, do-gooders and reformists? The Dandy is less cynical than the cynicism of that naive conviction. He deliberately chooses sterile protest without consequence.

Because naturally and at the same time strangely enough the Dandy protests—not literally, perhaps not even consciously, certainly not as a deliberate program. His attitude points to a paradox in the new society, in modernity. That paradox is that equality is a leveling out, not differentiation. Under the rule of equality, difference appears to melt away, and individuality atrophies. The Dandy parries this situation by reversing it: he makes a resounding difference by "perfectly" executing the rules of equality, to the point of absurdity, right through to its ultimate conclusion. He shows a kind of perfection that is banned by a society of equals: perfection is, after all, antidemocratic. At the same time, it obeys the social rule and is therefore unchallengeable. Excellence in conformism, provocatively obedient, in short a provocative work-to-rule.

That the Dandy's main task is throwing himself into outward appearance is a shocking waste. The male uniform is efficient, but that efficiency becomes a baroque ritual in the hands of the Dandy. He shamelessly adopts women's time-consuming way of getting dressed. He spares neither money nor time in weighing nuances and details that no one sees. Investment and result are out of balance: he wastes his effort in protest against the all-pervasive norm of efficiency.

Color

The color he wears is black. The color of mourning, as noted by de Musset and, many years later, Baudelaire. Mourning because men are no longer allowed to participate in the game of the imaginary body? In a mere two generations men renounce the sartorial imagination of the ancien régime. Men enter the straitjacket of the austere "costume"—the three-piece suit, the creation of puritan austerity, of classicist reduction to the elementary. One basic form, with a small range of fabrics and colors. Perfection within those limits presupposes extreme sophistication and a practiced eye to tell the difference.

Black is also the color of Manet, who studied it in Velázquez and the Dutch masters, both from the seventeenth century. The golden ages of flamboyant black: fiery and dramatic. And the classic men's suit is perhaps not the straitjacket at all but on the contrary the most revolutionary synthesis in the entire human history of fashion: smoothly adapted to the body, explicit about physique and limbs, sliding along with all movements in a practical way. The austere costume is a uniform, but its "Doric" clarity is also irresistible. Men are not only confined in it, but it is also an expression of their most masculine ideals.

Women

As a rule, the Dandy is *célibataire* and sometimes, but certainly not as a rule, homosexual. The Dandy actively polemicizes against women. They meet in front of the mirror, where both spend many hours of the day; neither wants to enter the street, that is, the social scene except with long, intense, and well-considered preparation and planning. For women, the mirror is already the gaze of the opposite sex; while for the Dandy the mirror is the merciless gaze of a much more abstract authority. He does not think of conquests but of humiliations. His appearance is the trap for the astonished other that he certainly does not want to see himself. At the same time, he knows that the street will not willingly submit to his "surprise" and will try to knock him off the pedestal at the slightest error. So the mirror must mercilessly reveal every weakness, every ridicule in advance. And he seems to have that mirror as company before him at all times, in the street, in the park: society is there only as a mirror. He is the Medusa who petrifies herself.

The Dandy is the heterosexual man who wards off women. After all, she is the Trojan horse that will tame masculinity rather than exalting it. Only declassified women will save him from sentimentality. Only women with make-up on are unnatural enough. For women are the principle of nature par excellence—their passions are real and therefore worthless to the Dandy. Nature is artless and therefore meaningless. The rising exaltation of nature by the bourgeoisie seems to him to be the ultimate stupidity. The Dandy knows that humans are not creatures of nature but creatures of culture. At the same time, women are fascinating because they are ambiguous and elusive, capricious and pure appearance. In this sense women realize his paradoxical ideal of the undefined in a way that is unattainable for the Dandy. But what women are by nature, the Dandy tries to deliberately realize as a life project.

Laughable

The Dandy is fundamentally laughable: from the point of view of women, from the point of view of citizens, from the point of view of proletarians. Everyone sees through his pretense, his sterile maneuvers, his frigidity. Everyone wonders what all this fuss is about, if it leads to no conquest, no gain. They couldn't care less whether the Dandy is haunted by a very old sense of honor. The Dandy lives by a code that is out of date. In a democracy there is no place for honor, only for profit margins.

Because society considers the code of honor as mere pretense, the Dandy can easily be exposed as pure masquerade. Consequently, he is a prominent figure in cartoons. After all, the Dandy is an image, a schematic concentration, a compressed formula. The changing nature of spontaneity—so well captured by photography—is alien to him. He has no surprises in store. He is—we would say today—exclusively an imago. His stylized form stands around a void. His appearance is a mask for a role: commedia dell'arte. Not that the Dandy is thrown off guard by any of that. He reverses his irrevocable feminization, his substantial superficiality, into as many proofs of a purely masculine bravado. The impossibility of his position and of his role makes him all the more impressive.

The Rhythm of Thinking[1]

Serge Daney[2] is the force of a surprising opening gambit. In the form of a question, or the negation of obviousness, as a rhyme of ideas or right away with a brutal argumentation that stalemates you, "if . . . then." The strategy of the brusque but also panicky outburst. The ground is not prepared, the argument not introduced. He parachutes the reader straight into the war zone. Bullets whiz around his ears, mines surround him. But the author says: I will lead you through it!

Reasoning will follow later. However narrow the road of the astonishing "attacco," he still leads you to ever wider views. He takes you spiraling along a mountain wall, higher and higher, with ever new and surprising connections. With this, too, he overwhelms you. You gasp for breath, you threaten to slide down, you lose your footing, but the writer uses your captivation to carve a way through your lazy obviousness.

Equally surprising is his coda: no conclusion but an open space into which you need to jump. He announces sequels, further developments, roads to travel. But you have understood by now that the writer is not a writer of closure, of panoramically looking back on the road traveled, of the finished labor of reasoning. He is not working on reasonings anyway; it is a never-ending moving up. Things do not follow logically but prismatically slide around each other.

He nevertheless manages to give this construction without an "introduction" or "conclusion" the character of a diamond. Not only with the ideas that have been conquered and created, but especially with the example that he gives of connections, with the style that he indicates of associations, with the coherence that he forces us to imagine between phenomena that we mindlessly (which is how it often seemed to me after having read a bit of Daney) accept. Do not, above all, accept anything, but resist and investigate it!

Daney is an intellectual program.[3] A program in the line of Bazin, Rivette, Bonitzer, that is to say a philosophical argument with (and not only about) film. Not regarding film as an object of study but as a philosophical subject. The film is not subjected to probing reflection from the outside, but the reflection occurs along with the matter, with the substance of the image, the montage, with the resistance of what is seen. For those who love both film and philosophy, the intimate entanglement of these two realms is particularly stimulating, adventurous and dramatic.

Time and again, I see professional philosophy and "essayism" nonchalantly pass this over. They do not perceive the arrangement's originality, nor the impulses that emanate from radically new images and signifying machines. Were it not for these few authors, the world in which film and television have become all-determining would appear to me as absolute delusion and anarchy. But they are here, and they allow for hand-to-hand combat with these prostheses of modern culture. This century is erroneously concerned with all kinds of avant-garde problems. To some, it has long been clear that our world is defined elsewhere.

Daney is a series of baffling defeats. He liquidates cinephilia; he has chronicled the demise of film in acrid distress calls. He has seen his intellectual program get kicked off the Cahiers premises like an old dog. And he has eventually seen himself sit down, dogged and bewildered, in front of the much maligned instrument of social control: television. While around him academic film studies all too efficiently accompanied cinema's dying process, he stubbornly refused to consider film as an object. He studied with it, he lived with it. Cinema remained the libidinous center of thought and life.

Somewhere, he diagnoses that the love of film often has to do with the absence of the father: the cinephile as a father orphan. The cinema as the dreamed home—a more perverse dream detour seems unimaginable. A place where passions can be peeped at onscreen, while in the auditorium everyone assumes a bachelor's autonomy. Both displacement and exaltation of a lifelong loss, of a life-structuring lack. There appears to be a structural relationship between the lack in the filmic organization and the libidinous lack of the father orphan. An Oedipal wound that can be repeated exaltingly in the film. The film is the ultimate beneficiary of all the homages generated by the perverse system; but the writer himself rumbles to the impasse of the machine in no time. "To try to hope desperately," Daney says about television. But his whole oeuvre, his most intimate style, the core of his "modus operandi" as a thinker, writer, polemicist, and inspirer, bears the stamp of despair, a despair without slowness and laziness, which excites and drives him at ever greater speed: productive despair, demanding despair. If everything is based on a misunderstanding, the freedom to justify is all the greater and the desire to do so all the more irrepressible. That which one cannot change, one must at least try to think.

III

Mise-en-Scène: The Most Beautiful Word about Film[1]

But alas, it is no longer used. People obviously still know the technical function of directing. But the aesthetic quality it once denoted? No. It is as if it has been cut out of film culture. No film critique that still uses the word, no audience that enjoys it, and hardly any films in which it can be seen.

For me, however, it remains the most beautiful word about film. It introduced me to true intimacy with films. It was the watchword of cinephilia. Observing the mise-en-scène gave all the other elements of a film their own vibrato. It is the source of an enthusiasm ("critical enthusiasm") that led not to an interpretative delirium ("what is meant") but to an affective delirium ("what is there to empathize with").[2,3]

Mise-en-scène is a particular form of directing. It was observed, made autonomous, and commented on by postwar French film criticism. André Bazin[4] used it in the *Revue du Cinema*, and later, in the *Cahiers du Cinéma*, it belonged to the standard film-critical vocabulary.

To speak of mise-en-scène is thus to speak of a historical phenomenon: as a term from the history of film criticism, as a way of making films (mostly in the 1940s and 1950s).

The history of postwar film criticism has yet to be written. Any reading of texts by Bazin and the *Cahiers* editors reminds the reader of the obvious fact that one cannot brand this tradition as "realism" and "auteur theory," as people have been doing for quite a while now. These are two far from uninteresting, yet highly speculative, notions that the French tradition of film criticism has been handling very imaginatively but never dogmatically. Besides, the mise-en-scène touched on so many more facets of film than would be apparent from these two notions. Hence my suggestion that the term "mise-en-scène" could shed a fascinating new light on a part of film culture that has been handled rather crudely.

In what follows, I would like to suggest some themes I am reminded of by the expression "mise-en-scène." A sketch of a pattern book, ideas about a word.

Labor

Simply put, mise-en-scène is the entire work performed on a film set: working with the set design, with props, with actors, with lighting, with sound, with the camera. Mise-en-scène is what one sees in Godard's *Contempt*, in Minnelli's *Two Weeks in Another Town*.[5]

Mise-en-scène is a labor process. On set, an intricate and subtle linkage of things, people and machines is established. The artisanal and the technological, the rigorously technical and the much more obscure creative working procedures are laboriously fitted together. There is a heterogeneity of labor cultures: the set craftsman, the creative concentration of the actor, the precise technology of the film equipment. They are labor cultures without a common language, brought together by the directing.

Mise-en-scène is a production process. The intricate linkage of the labor process must result in a unique, one-off product, namely that one specific film shot. Immediately afterwards, everything is taken down and reconstructed into a different linkage.

Mise-en-scène as an aesthetic category has to do with the awareness of this unique character of each film shot. Mise-en-scène is the negation of film production as serial production. It is the emphasis on a permanent state of inspired bricolage. Every film shoot is a triumph over its improbability. "Mise-en-scène is putting something together, which can be said to be well or badly put together."[6,7]

Watching and appreciating a film starting from its mise-en-scène is like adding a fourth dimension to plot and characters. Behind the characters their maker appears, behind the plot the process of the mise-en-scène appears.

This addition pulls the film open. A gap emerges, a margin. It has become a point of doctrine to interpret that opening as a distancing, as dissociation, alienation, objectification, criticism. These are the form-stylistic and later the content-ideological ways in which people have sought to interpret the mise-en-scène. Already the *Cahiers* critics themselves said that the Hollywood material is trivial and that style there is a superior treatment, or a coded critique of it.

This seems to me to be a modernist appropriation of the mise-en-scène. It fits too well into a conception of art plagued by permanent self-interrogation, into a so-called critical approach to the culture industry.

Reading some of the key texts on mise-en scène, one notices that in those texts it creates no distance whatsoever, serves no self-protective reflex.[8] On the contrary, the mise-en-scène functions as exaltation. It deepens, intensifies, radicalizes. It is the ultimate sign of a deep solidarity with the material. Mise-en-scène is not the place of doubt, but of rapture.

There is a second facet to this distorted, detached interpretation of mise-en-scène, namely that it would be a way of emphasizing the shooting situation. Mise-en-scène as visible, emphasized labor. In this, one misses the essential maneuvers of the mise-en-scène. For the mise-en-scène may well make the shooting situation autonomous, but it is also a (visible!) step back. Against the standard decoupage, the metteur-en-scène sets a certain contemplativeness. His presence manifests itself through emphatic restraint (which of course is not the removal of manipulation and labor, but a different form of it). One sees the metteur-en-scène as a figure stretched between two extremes: enthusiasm and restraint, solidarity and distance. The entire mise-en-scène as an aesthetic issue rests on the paradoxical combination of passive and active, absence and intervention, doing and letting it happen. The mise-en-scène does not serve a clear, identifiable, demonstrable meaning—it does not clarify, does not critique. If anything, it distrusts meaning, tries to outwit it.

Physical

In film, everything that cannot be shown is abstract: motives, points of view, psychology, connections, and explanations; in short, a considerable part of the machinery of the well-told story. Mise-en-scène is opposed to everything that is abstract, giving the concrete a more intense form of presence.

Everything in film has a double form of that presence (each with its own "weight"): the presence of being in the image and that of being narratively motivated. In the mise-en-scène, the presence in the image prevails; it distrusts any presence motivated by story or decoupage.

This does not mean that the story is disdained. It is merely told and used differently by the mise-en-scène. The strict narrative logic is carefully bypassed, very gently put into perspective. It is suggested that it could be not the purpose but merely an alibi. And the distinct emotions of each scene are pushed to the fore. The mise-en-scène emphasizes the states, the modes of being, the qualities of the situation (which are abstractions too, but of a different nature from the narrative ones). Narrative elements are starting places, not for a sequence, but for a brutal explosion of emotions, or an irresistible blossoming of them.

Mise-en-scène treats story elements a bit like opera does with its arias: there is a story, but on top of that there are drawn-out and spun-out expressions of the emotions of that situation.

Mise-en-scène is very often very baroque, expressionistic, even hysterical. It is certainly no coincidence that the *Cahiers* thematized it during the 1950s. This baroque film decade brought the mise-en-scène to fruition as a trope.

This form was erroneously given a realistic meaning. The asceticism with regard to the narrative, combined with gluttony with regard to the visible, resulted in a very affected parti-pris. I cannot help but feel that the mise-en-scène functions as a dandyish reflex. Facing the banally visible not with the weapons of meaning but with those of style is rather like the cross-grained ambition of dandies. For them, too, meaning (content) is tasteless and vulgar as a defense against reality. For them, too, only one thing matters: the allure with which one touches the concrete.

Mise-en-scène is touching, where feeling is limited to showing and showing already has the insistence of feeling. And here I should quote Astruc: "What is seen is less important, not than how it is seen, but than a certain way of needing to see and show."[9]

The Visual

The stakes of the mise-en-scène are badly understood if one presents it as a visual style, as plastic forms on the screen, as something pictorial. It is not an art of the beautiful but of the intelligent image ("The idea of a thing never ceases to run underneath that thing without the need to abandon it").[10, 11]

The mise-en-scène and the "politique des auteurs" [auteur theory] are badly understood if one remains blind to the enormous significance of the nineteenth-century romantic with its double-entry bookkeeping of coolly registering, in which both myth and pathos seem to find their place.

Mise-en-scène is a blessed moment in film history that realizes endless play, a never-stabilizing balancing act between opposing demands and options. No wonder that, in the tradition of film criticism, they did not hesitate to place the mise-en-scène at the level of spirituality. Not spirituality as a realm of meaning but as the essence of a will, an obsession, and an intellect. Here, all meaning is fuel for a style: how one places oneself and the level at which one does so.

The Classic Film Body[1]

That something has changed is apparent, at least for me, from the caution with which I surround my increasingly rare visits to the cinema today. The relationship of trust is gone; my expectations no longer match the offerings. So I am not surprised by the hypothesis that there is something fundamentally new at stake in film. That this novelty has to do with the body seems obvious to me. For me, film has long been first and foremost the bizarre art of showing and looking at bodies, the art of inventing hundreds of ways in which emotions and consciousness become bodily visible. Film is narration through bodies rather than images. Images are at the service of those bodies, are draped around those bodies, filled with bodies, carried by bodies. When film changes, it does so in what I call "the image body," which is what is at stake in any rearrangement. In case of radical change (as with the introduction of sound film), everything is rearranged around that body: different lighting, a different frame, a different way of cutting images together, a different diegetic space, but also a different way of placing the spectators around that body, a different way of giving them a place in the image. In short, it is an entire chain of quasi-contractual relations that suddenly changes.

It is only when this body has changed that it becomes possible to contemplate the earlier body, which has been put out of action. Only then does the classic film body become visible, nameable because it is no longer self-evident. Study demands the absence of what is studied. Enthusiastic reflection, but at the same time a mourning process. In its evocation, what is remembered hears its own ebbing away.

When film changes, the old becomes visible—in the new, opposite the new, from the new. The two are diametrically opposed and yet fundamentally connected. Knowledge of one is only possible through knowledge of the other, and vice versa. Knowledge of the old in turn allows knowledge of the new. The conflict seems fruitful.

Old and New

To weigh the new image against the old one, I am restricting myself to two aspects: the affective distance between the image and the spectator and the type of credibility peculiar to the new image.

About this distance: the video and television image is intended for practical, close-up, intimate, and careless use. It is a piece of furniture filling the house, not a collective phenomenon. The cinema was a temple, the film a moment of adoration, a fundamentally elevating event. Everyone knows the distinction: one looks up at the screen in the cinema, one looks down at the screen of video and television. That looking down has to do with the simple placement of the screen across from the viewer, but the difference in spatiality is also already saying something about affect and its grammar. That spatial arrangement literally and figuratively determines a relationship.

Because of the condescending relationship, a kind of countermovement occurs from the side of the screen: a provocative revenge. Between television and the audience, there is distrust, disdain, deep and fundamental animosity. The classic film body offered itself without reserve, generous, revealing, obscene (if you like), to the generous, receptive, naive (if you like) spectator. The new film body is modeled on the condescending attitude toward television; it is frugal with its outpourings, suspicious of its own vulnerability, distrustful of the spectator. The new film body, unlike the classic film body's uniformity, is complex, layered, split and fundamentally unhappy with that.

There is a second dimension to the new film's radical difference from the old one: the kind of image we see on the screen. In the first hundred years of the medium's history, it was a photographic image. There was an analogy between the image and what was depicted due to the photographic printing technique of both photography and film. The images were created in a camera, a black box that did not involve the hand of a creator. The new image, which is electronic and thus manipulable in the depth below what is visible, no longer has ontological evidential force: it is a fundamentally manipulated and constructed image. It is a trick, no longer an appearance: the spectators have a playful, noncommittal relation to this image body. How would they invest themselves in it? It is a noncommittal screen appearance! What could they gain from investing as spectators? Surely they can only be deceived! The great classic film bodies, those of glamour and Method, of neorealism and modern improvisation, Eisenstein's attraction-body and the fascinating document-body of cinema vérité, all rely on that overwhelming ontological credibility, which was indubitable. That doubt has effortlessly and harmlessly become our new certainty.

The Classic Film Body

The classic film body is carried by a kind of relationship of faith between the image and the spectator, and it supports that relationship. This regime of faith gives the film body impressive room for expansion—how reckless and boundless that body seems!

It explores the space of the spectator relationship in all directions. The playing around this regime is endlessly varied: from the playing in comedies and melodramas to Astaire's improbable dancing and Hitchcock's stiff model. It is so very different each time, and that difference is an essential part of film history and culture, determining its likes and dislikes. The body that has to play in this regime of faith is of course supported in this by the direction, mise-en-scène and montage. Yet, above all, the body itself must embody this complex game of credibility. As spectators, we unconsciously but very intensely coexperienced the pleasure of that game for a hundred years. The body did not primarily play a role—action and emotion—but above all played a game with that credibility. The body was not present in a depicting way but it created being: it made the spectator and the image be a certain way. Watching this image body, the spectator went through all movements of faith of acting. When that faith in the image, and thus in the body that is seen in that image, is lost, the relationship to the film image fundamentally deteriorates. The spectators no longer engage their "being" but only the ability to receive information. That information is not subject to questions of faith. From now on, what occurs on the new screen is a fact without references to anything whatsoever. That is simply the consequence of the possibility of image manipulation. The image is no longer the result of an engagement of reality in the filming and therefore no longer demands an engagement from the viewer. It even excludes that engagement.

The one-dimensional flatness of contemporary actors, of the image body they help create, deprives cinema of an essential dimension. That lack, however, is compensated for. After all, why go to the cinema if there is nothing left to experience? The actor slides away from the center of the film image to the position of instrument or (raw) material of the image, like food to be masticated. It is essential that actors can be worked in and by the new film image. Their metamorphosis is central (but it is not the actors who are metamorphosing, but rather the image that is metamorphosing through them). The new actor must be recomposable—which is by the way an ancient and fundamental dream of the entire film history and its fascination with all kinds of trickery (montage being the first and most crucial of all tricks). Although the montage that sets image against image is just an old-fashioned primal form of trickery that intervenes in the image, in its physical continuity.

The classic film body is essentially expressive: it concerns emotions. Emotions presuppose a complex landscape of the internal and the external, of behavior and reaction, as well as a fixed link between the two. Differentiation in this makes up the individuality of a character, the style of an actor. In the new body, however, emotion is not a lived category but a programmed one, less an inner than an outer characteristic. Emotions are of the same order as hair color, thumbprint, DNA structure: they are not what you are, but what can betray you. You have them because you belong to the species, but at the same time they are your handicap. This particularity makes you less interchangeable and therefore less flexibly employable. The current film body says "I" by way of computer arrangement. No unique way of being is constructed around such an "I" anymore—certainly not by the psychological patterns used to construct positions into persons. The "I" has literally become a pure shifter; it belongs to nobody.

The most interesting question is nevertheless: what will film look like without emotions in their classical function? How do you show a character in which the "I" no longer fulfills a grammatically orienting function? After all, all classic film language revolves around the construction and exploitation of that "I position" in the image body. That is where all the threads of scenario, direction, acting, montage, and spectators converge. That is what the spectators talk about afterward, what they identify with, what they sympathize with, what entices them into moral judgments and statements.

Inevitably, such a new film construction has far-reaching consequences for the film language, for the construction of the image. The question of those consequences can activate viewing, trace a new kind of attention, send reflection back to the concrete film material. The question forces the radically new-seeming film to account for its ways of being and doing—before the century-old tribunal of film history, until further notice. After all, these are the new tenants of a respectable house. The testates of *La Maison Cinéma*[2] have every reason to ask about the young tenants' intentions. If only for the sake of form.

Seam and Pattern: Thinking Forms[1]

Pourquoi couper un plan?
[*Why cut a shot?*]
—Jean-Luc Godard

The pattern is a collection of paper shapes, with lines and symbols in pencil. It looks like a puzzle, with parts that are sometimes recognizable as figures but often are not. They are intriguing because they offer a glimpse behind the scenes. They surprise by the complexity of shapes that are needed to make a jacket or a dress. The garment that we recognize and take in at a glance as a whole falls apart in the pattern into a bizarre collection of often unrecognizable fragments. The projection of the dress on a flat surface leads to strange distortions. The skeleton in our bodies and the textile skeleton around our bodies seem barely related. But we live in mannerist times, aesthetically sensitive to the language of deformation. The pattern provides an ancient and venerable version of this, which until now has rarely been tested for its aesthetic capital.

The pattern has a complex status. At its core, it is a practical aid that belongs in studios and production halls. It is the matrix of a design so that it can be faithfully executed—in a few or in countless copies. Besides, in the pattern lies the core of a design on the basis of which copyrights can be claimed.

The pattern reveals something about clothing and fashion that we easily overlook. For even though clothing is a fundamental part of the arts of movement (dance, film, but also martial arts), the pattern reminds us that it also an *art de l'espace*, an art of space, akin to architecture and figurative sculpture. The pattern as a distinct figurative architecture. Yet there is a compelling, essential unity between the movement of walking—so essential in fitting—and the space in which one learns to walk in a new dress. The interferences between a men's suit and space, between a stage and a dance costume, are so essential that a distinction seems out of place. It seems impossible to distinguish between the pattern (as a form of space) and the dress (as a form of movement). Yet there is the stimulating and unbridgeable distance between *Vogue* and *Burda*[2], between the pattern file of the Dior company and its fashion photograph by Maywald, between Romy Schneider in a Chanel suit and the work table on which the paper pattern was spread out to be cut out of the fabric. The contradiction and unity of being dressed and pattern, that is what this essay is about.

The Pattern as a Working Tool

The creation of the pattern is an intermediate step, a technical aid with the status of a protocol. It contains information on how to proceed; it is a production process, a manual. The pattern is not an invitation to look, but to do. In the pattern a course of action is plotted out; in the sharp outlines a virtual hand is already at work.

Here, however, we are only stimulated to look, in the way we might look at exhibited architectural and machine drawings, at the plates of the *Encyclopédie*. We see a technical way of thinking at work that as unintentionally as inevitably generates its own beauty. The beauty of those plans strikes us all the more today because structuring as such is considered an eminently human activity in our time, *the* cultural modus operandi.

The pattern is a practical tool—like the screenplay for the film director, the negative for the photographer, the gridded background drawing for the painter, the architectural plan for the builder. All are *en amont* [upstream] the result of creative design and *en aval* [downstream] that which must be realized. The negative is already entirely the photograph, the script the film, the background drawing the painting, and at the same time it is not a film, not a photograph, not a painting at all. The unfilmed script is everything, and yet not a film at all. The design as such hardly has any value but it is far from worthless. Similarly, the pattern allows a dress to be made completely and accurately, without even remotely being the dress. The pattern is the core, but at the same time it is unreal: it has yet to be realized, just as one says of shooting a movie.

Contemplating a Craft

Contemplating the pattern is thinking about a *technè*—a working process, a "way of making," a *métier*. But there is substantial incommensurability between the technique of thinking and the technique of making. The tools of thinking aim to separate, to distinguish. Thinking sharply is recognizing differences where others see no difference because they make no distinction. The tools of making, on the other hand, are aimed at bringing together, connecting. Against the distinguishing movement of thinking, the connecting movement of making.

Thinking always installs a homogeneous plane for thinking: only what is relevant is reserved for thinking. Making, on the other hand, aims precisely to connect the nonhomogeneous: pure thinking versus impure making. Thinking makes general statements, making looks for a new, unique solution for each situation. Thinking applies norms, making looks at the result without principle. Thinking about craftsmanship implies a contradiction, because the better one is able to categorize *métier*, the less one understands it. As a rule, practical solutions are a far cry from theoretical ones. Categorical understanding often doesn't benefit the hands and eyes, quite the contrary.

This difficulty can be applied to the relationship between a pattern-maker and a designer. The latter brings sketches to a design, with samples of fabric, color indications, atmospheric suggestions. His proposal is a tangle of heterogeneous elements that nevertheless immediately form a whole. The patternmaker must think this synthetic proposal into pattern terms: how do I put it together, and how do I take apart the overall idea first in order to do this? The patternmaker must translate it into fragments, seams, and points. Visually, the result is very different from the original design. Yet the pattern is a necessary tool for realizing the design.

Both movements—designing and pattern drawing—come together again during the fitting: has the pattern drawer's thinking really thought the designer's idea, that is, thought its realization and feasibility, its viability?

Model-Thinking: Selection, Projection, and Scale

The pattern belongs to the family of model-thinking. The pattern does not reproduce (like, say, a model drawing), but "modelizes." Three tactics are of importance here: selection, projection, and scale. The map is a good example.

Depending on the intention of the map, this or that element is included or omitted: selection. A map is not a photograph but a filtering. In the pattern, everything that might convince the buyer is omitted, leaving only that which helps and guides the making.

The pattern resembles a cadastral map; the patternmaker is the surveyor of dress. The pattern does not translate a visual impression but very sharply sets out the geometrical realities of distances and proportions in a precise description of materials. Just as the cadastral map is not a roadmap but the accurate measurement of land parcels, so the pattern is a sharp measurement of all the necessary pieces. The pattern is at once also a production manual, like the electrical diagram of a house. Some aspects of the pattern look figurative and analog but it is also largely a system of signs with conventional symbols for buttons, stitches, folds, and notches. Each pattern is accompanied by an implicit legend, like a map is accompanied by the conventional symbols for roads, railroads, waterways, contour lines.

The model is a labor protocol: follow those steps and you will arrive at the intended result, like a cookbook, a darkroom manual, the operating manual for an appliance. The model is a score, a dialogue. Throughout the making process, the text indicates, "First this . . . and then that . . ." In the hands of a tailor, the pattern unfolds into a working process across time. Like the construction of a house that is followed with fascination, a costume is put together step by step. That process is contained in the pattern, like a tree in a seed.

"Modelizing" is also projection. The pattern projects a three-dimensional object on a plane. Often it is even more complicated: the pattern translates a two-dimensional design back into a plane, but in order to do that, it is necessary first to imagine a three-dimensional version of that design. Only then can the pattern be plotted.

Projection is not creative interpretation; it must be a flawlessly precise conversion, from one currency into another, without any loss whatsoever. Projection aspires to equivalence: one is worth the other, one can be converted into the other and vice versa.

The projection surface is the beautiful tracing paper. It is of a warm yellow, "crackles" and rustles (it makes a sound you can immediately tell from all other kinds of paper), feels dry and looks greasy, is opaque (not transparent) but glowingly translucent. The graphite of the pencil adheres to its fine pores as sensually as melted butter. When you tear it, you see that it is thick and fibrous. In the tracing paper, the fibers break; they leave a white break line. In the fabric, on the other hand, the fibers do not break but keep bending. Placing tracing paper is a very different operation from placing fabric on the sewing table. Tracing paper never falls down into a drape; it almost remains stiff as you lift it. The combination of tracing paper and textiles in the studio is a delightfully tactile feast.

The pattern on tracing paper is pinned to the fabric—just as a model drawing leaves charcoal marks on the freshly applied fresco via tiny perforations. For a moment, the tracing paper is pinned to the fabric. Then the scissors translate the pattern shape into fabric. This way, there are two versions of the pattern pieces: in paper and in fabric. The first version is the result of calculation and drawing, the second belongs immediately to the textile acts: needle and thread, "needlework." There is a paradigm shift here—between the crackling paper and the soundless fabric—with very different sensibilities. Paper belongs to the world of drawing and writing, of calculated rescaling, of extremely precise construction, like assembling a clockwork. The labor of the patternmaker is intellectual, mathematical. One mustn't come forward with vague suggestions but with practicable, repeatable solutions.

The fabric, on the other hand, with which the seamstress makes the toile and later the final version, has a specific texture which one first reads in tactile way. The fabric is like earth with an endless variation of loam or sand, from sticky to grainy—the seamstress plows through the fabric. Abstract, calculated solutions do not suffice here; each time, a tactile compromise with the fiber structure must be sought. Therefore, one does not sew a vest together mechanically but rather puts it together by feeling and trying. The pattern pieces are not serially put together but like a composition.

Projection always occurs to scale. Projection is not a print through contact, but a calculated, converted copy. Hence the possibility of enlarging—like a photogram of a few square centimeters converted into tens of square meters of image on a film screen—but also of scaling down—like the eighteenth-century mannequin, which Gainsborough, for example, had in his studio.

The pattern, however, does not seize the opportunity of changing dimension. Between the pattern as a projection and the garment, the ratio is 1:1. Scale manifests itself elsewhere, namely when grading, when adapting to different sizes. The design is plotted in a range of sizes. With the mechanization and industrialization of ready-to-wear, the demand for an orderly typology of sizes and for standardized procedures for their adjustment has become mathematized knowledge. In pattern books, the visual result of these diagrams and calculations is always fascinating—their vague kinship with Marey's analyses of movement offers food for thought.

"Tailor-made" indicates the tension between the generality of the design and the particularity of each body buying the garment in a specific size. Between the general visual proposal of a model and the one-off size lies an intriguing gap to be resolved by the patternmaker. The design is sizeless, actually, and the patternmaker analyzes it into a schematic ensemble of parts but must also be able to further project the pattern onto the range of sizes. The pattern designer thus makes a number of sliding transitions from the design to the unruly, obstinate body of the client. In this sense, the patternmaker is at once a metaphor for any awareness of and handling the concrete: healing and loving, teaching and exercising power, creating beauty and growing fruit. Each time abstract ideas must be put into practice. Everywhere that wonderful alchemy of the general and the specific.

The fitting of the toile—a first rendition of the pattern in muslin— demonstrates this logic in a very explicit way. A mannequin is invited to put on this first version based on the pattern: how does this pattern version hang? The designer's idea and the patternmaker's technical interpretation of it can only be verified and adjusted on a living body. It is like a film dialogue that reads beautifully on paper but must in the end feel right in the mouth of the actor: usually that dialogue must be rewritten in accordance with the mouth of the actor. That indeterminable margin of verification, compromise, and deliberation, peculiar to this performing phase, discourages humans who think abstractly and want to be able to use clear categories. The interplay between body and design, between patternmaker and designer, between fabric and form, between draping and seam is to the outsider discouragingly elusive and therefore banal. Or, indeed, fascinating because of the multiplicity and complexity of factors deployed simultaneously with such spontaneity and practical success.

The Hilarious Pattern

To the textile worker the pattern is a schematic work tool, but to the spectator it looks like a caricature. It is blank as a child's drawing or an informative graph. It lies open as a fossil, it is pieced together like a jumping jack. Some parts are recognizable, others take on grotesque dimensions; they are wild deformations that would fit a fantasy creature.

The pattern is unintentionally hilarious with its unexpected hall-of-mirror-like widening and narrowing. Some plastic passages look like extremely mannerist complications. Just as an anatomical plate illuminates the skin and exposes the muscles and organs in thin layers that fan out, so too the patternmaker makes nothing less than an anatomical analysis of the design. Compared to the couturier's design or to later fashion drawings or photographs, the pattern is a sinister dismantling from which all movement has disappeared to the benefit of a clinical and hierarchical fragmentation.

The pattern keeps to the middle between the recognizability of the human figure (neck, arms, legs) and barely recognizable deformations (for dresses and panels). Usually, deformations compress; in the pattern, they mostly fan out. The figure projected in the clothing is smeared out like a liquid; the dresses fold out like the giant wings of tiny bats. The pattern vibrates between recognition and alienation, between form and distortion, between the proximity of the body and the distance of a pre-historic organism.

Therefore, the pattern is not skin but packaging. Just as wrapping paper is many times larger than what is wrapped, so the pattern covers a much larger area than the skin that has to be covered. There is always so much more fabric needed than skin. In Ribera's painting *Apollo and Marsias* (1637), there are two pieces of fabric: while Marsias's stripped-off skin is a red rag that is pulled from his leg, there is a vast red cloth flapping in the wind around the serene Apollo. The skin of Marsias is close-fitting, the cloth of Apollo an overwhelming and gen-erous volume. Similarly, the patternmaker mediates between skin and cloth, between biological nature and breathable draping, which is myth-ically indeterminate.

I remember the subtle sadism with which my mother transferred the *Burda* pattern onto fabric, with needles and a white fabric pencil. She cut it, draped it around my sister's back and took it back off again. For a moment, fabric and back were one: a dressed girl. Then the fabric, pieced together with needles, hung between my mother's fingers, like a limp milk skin on a teaspoon.

Also in Christian Schad's famous *Self-Portrait with Model* (1927), a lot is told through fabric. A ribbon knotted into a bracelet, a translu-cent curtain, crumpled sheets after sex, a purple checkered blanket, a red stocking around her thigh. But above all, the transparent green shirt through which the painter showed off his hairy chest and nipples, with an open collar buttoned with a lace. Right in that buttoned collar, the coquettishly transparent silk tilts into green skin that has been stitched up. This association is all the more irresistible because she has a wide scar on her face with six sutures. In Ribera, in Schad, and in my child-hood memories, the "needlework" configuration takes on an unsettling dimension.

The Splice

No pattern, either for draping or skin. Pattern presupposes a desire to impose a construction on textiles or to mark the skin. Draping is lim-ited to a buckle and a belt; the fabric is wrapped, folded back, pleated, and knotted. No permanent intervention takes place—each draping is unique, each form is free and therefore shapeless.

How different are sewn garments. The seam is like the truss of a roof, like the rigging of a sailing ship. Its construction lines are the masts, or poles, with attachment points and circus-tent cables. At first the canvas lies flat and crumpled on the lawn, then the poles go up and the canvas stretches triumphantly into a panting volume. Similarly, the seamstress lifts the fabric along seams and points, by cutting and stitching, so that the fabric fills with volume. Just as the ship's sail rises and the wind bil-lows the sails, humans wear textiles, billowed not only by his body, but also by his temperament and passions. Just as the inner self expresses itself in dress, the human skeleton is inside the body and the seams are the textile skeleton on the outside.

Draping is a dash of fabric, with narrowings and widenings, locks and waterfalls, deltas and stagnant tributaries. Draping unfolds the fabric by compressing it at strategic moments. The sash is one of the last objects where our clothing lets us play with that pouring of fabric. One knots the sash to secure it so as to let the two tails hang loose. Draped textiles are pure energy. We can put a frivolous rulelessness into it.

How different is cut fabric, stretched precisely within the seam, as if in a torturing tensile machine. Not generous textile but a measured construction with as little fabric loss as possible. Not a negligee, but a *serré*. Draped fabric hangs; cut fabric is tightened in the seam. The seam is where the energy of draping is converted into the tension of a construction. The energy flow of the fabric spread out on the work table is reduced to a local concentration of energy, an accumulation of tension and force. There is always tension, both when wearing and looking at a vest or pants—high tension even. The patternmaker places, regulates, and doses that tension. The designer's sketch suggests a certain intensity and distribution of tension which must be installed by the patternmaker very precisely. There is a specific "énergie Chanel," just as there is a specific "energia Armani."

That seam resembles the splice of a film editor. The transition from one image to another helps the narration, but it does so in a particular way, with greater or lesser energy, with a surprising jump cut or an elegant continuity. The editor's *Schnitt* is not a cutting away but a cutting together. In a pattern, too, cutting away is not an end in itself but the condition for a stitching together. In both cases, cutting is joining; the *coupure*'s fragmentation is the couture showing through. The place where the splice, the seam, is put, determines the energy and thus the soul of the garment. Where you put the seam is—as in film—a technical but at the same time always an aesthetic and sensual choice.

The seam is the signature line of the design. The seam is one of the many manifestations of the line that are constitutive of clothing. The line of draping is unrepeatable and permanently in motion. The line of the pattern, on the other hand, is fixed; so it is crucial where you put it. That line is not the inspiration of the wearer but of the designer. The line is stitched and fixed. It is the designer's *griffe* [signature stamp, label]; the tattooing of the textile. Even in the design drawing, even in the fashion drawing, even in the pose of a mannequin in front of a fashion photographer or in the terminology of the silhouette, the theme of the line recurs. Wearing a garment is essentially wearing a line. This dramatic line full of character is a beautiful translation of the art of movement expressed in clothing. The line of the designer indicates a certain speed, a certain style of movement, which can be seen so purely but also fleetingly in the free draping. The line is a fixed, simplified and above all hardened draping.

In pattern drawing, however, the line is not to be found: its cadastral, geometric character is stripped of energy, aggression, character, temperament. Yet the pattern line is the condition for the ferocity with which *la griffe* defines the soul of a design. The lines of pattern drawing form a network of intersecting tight angles and arcs. This analytical representation of the draping seam line in the fabric shows that the pattern belongs to an entirely different paradigm: that of machine construction, not of the working of a machine.

When fitting the toile, you can see how the designer's work balances between the line of the design and the fitting line imposed on it by the mannequin's body. Two kinds of gestures mark the difference between those two lines: the caressing, gently tapping gesture that is used to properly hang the garment—the draping gesture of fitting—and on the other hand, the mostly horizontal, sharp gestures, cutting and going against the hanging fabric. This is the line of the seam, of the *Schnitt*. The first gesture responds to the model's unique body; in the second gesture the logic of the design is set against the body. Between the caressing and the angular lies the direction of the textile by the designer. Relentless and supple, measured cutting and loose kneading. The way great directors treat their actors.

Paper Dolls

The pattern speaks the same language as the box of blocks, as Lego, Meccano, and Kapla. The pieces scream to be lined up. But what I find most related are the chromolithographs with figures, garments, and objects, preprinted and to be cut out. You had to pay particular attention to tabs and slots, because that's where the suturing happened later. That dogged effort to follow the cutting line so very precisely! That curiosity to transform the little girls and guys by putting on and taking off hats, pants, dresses, shoes, and vests! The delight of that game feels like yesterday. In the paper patterns to be cut out and put together, I enjoyed the making side of sartorial illusions and conventions. I only had to turn my figure over to see the folding and pasting on which the nice front was based—there was nothing more to it. Not out of desire for disenchantment, which is alien to children, but for the giddiness of swinging between the shiny front and matte back, between pretty and seam, between real and gone. Today, in the pattern's inside-out, I experience the same giddiness—a miscellany of epistemological and erotic confusion.

The fashion print has maintained a much closer connection with the childlike passion for pattern thinking than fashion photography. In the latter, the models push me precisely out of the childlike. They recalibrate my libido and direct me to the game of eroticism, away from the much deeper game of illusionistic creation that touches the core of consciousness.

The pattern speaks to the childlike passion for fantasy play. It is akin to puppetry, to the pleasure of making a fantasy world rather than looking at it. The tailor's passion is quite different from that of the wearer of clothes. The former produces illusions, the latter experiences them. It is a different entrance to illusion. But the designer and the patternmaker use different entrances, too. The former is rather like a screenwriter and director of the social, through dress. The latter is rather like the puppeteer who, with threads and distorted voices, is more fascinated by the magic of creating illusions than by the illusion conjured up, more by the artifice than by the spectacle.

A Philosophy of Making

Looking into the workshop—of a cook, a photographer, an editor, or a tailor—is always the beginning of a voyage of discovery with unsuspected vistas. Every "Why do you do that?" is later followed by a questioning, "What does what you do mean?"

If a profession (but it can also be a domestic task) is always and above all a succession of routines, bound by matter and conventions, it is also always a revelatory place about the ingenuity of a tradition that gives form to textiles, taste to food, rhythm and legibility to a succession of images. The intimate, practical knowledge of things and tools—such as the use of language and words—always holds the utopian promise of a deeper, true knowledge. A knowledge of things as they really are because they have been tested by hands and experienced by users. Again and again, the logic of making and the more hidden logic of using seem to hold the keys to a soft, applied, and lived philosophy. A philosophy that would pass through doing, that holds out the prospect of a thinking way of doing. In which ultimately not language but the hand would be the philosophical instrument par excellence. The dream of the ultimate materialistic philosophy.

Dreaming of an Expedition[1]

1.

The nineteenth century invents exoticism and makes it readily available. Through countless optical devices, the alien has come ever closer. The alien in which one is unfaithful: to one's own fate, one's own sex, one's spouse, one's own country, one's own culture. Our century selected film as the instrument of that exotic adventure. An adventure that, if not over, certainly seems to have begun a whole new cycle.

Exoticism puts you elsewhere, shifts you, rearranges the relations between body and imagination, between looking and knowing, between the consciousness of something outside oneself and self-consciousness. The entire substance of the psychological apparatus, the entire weight of the moral and factual order of things is tilting. Not into a revolutionary, once again definitive recalibration, but into something that remains provisional, inconsistent and halfhearted. Film changes everything and leaves everything untouched. It is the realm par excellence of what is doubtful, dubious. With this kind of slipping, film drives a wedge between the certainties of the world.

(Film is indeed always the other country—America, France, Italy. It is a way of traveling, of seeing how people live elsewhere, how they do so in other landscapes, other houses and cities. Wearing other clothes, with strangely unfamiliar ways of moving their bodies, with other sounds and intonations to express their feelings. It is a permanent world exhibition, an inexhaustible encyclopedia in which nothing ever becomes banal.)

2.

The temporarily abandoned boy looks at a projection in his grand-parents' home. A beloved uncle stretches a canvas, dims the room and makes boyish jokes as he starts up a prehistoric wooden box from which light bursts out with roaring violence, making moving figures (Chaplin?) flop down onto the sheet. He did not see the depth of the image as much as the flat projection on the canvas.

The slightly less abandoned boy sits down with the grandfather on wooden chairs in a school to watch a film about Spain, *Alcatraz*.[2] He sees action, dust, explosions, sweat, suffering, and death. He sees a story.

The boy goes to the big city with his father to see a Schneider film. He is in love. On the way back, his father searches his soul: to observe infatuation, as in a small cinema? The boy has seen a beautiful woman whose lips, when talking, move him to this very day. He understands (but does not accept) that she came so close to him but that he has to stay so far away from her.

Three phases: the image, the story, the woman. A few more films. A few more impasses and life has put him in the position of the one who prefers the dark room, the distant image, the kitschy melodrama over all the temptations of reality. Fortunately, there was film. To love film—he discovered much later—is to be in oedipal impasses without which film is at best mere entertainment. (When a culture, through a changed family structure and gender relations, slightly rearranges the oedipal adventure, doesn't the role and place of film change as well? Isn't a certain fascination for film irrevocably a product of its time?)

3.

The cinema was his America, the images followed one another like solemn seven-league strides, like running the hundred meters. He shifted from place to place, from one figure to another. And it always happened within that exact distance. Without realizing it, film pulled him into a partner dance. Later, he understood that everything revolved around an oxymoron: to be moved unmovingly.

But in the cinema, all emotions are experienced exclusively inside oneself (one watches inside one's head in the same way that one starts to read in silence). The immobility of a cinema audience is terrifying. Their complete lack of expression looks downright dumb, like people watching the landing in *Close Encounters*...

Film was an empty theater, during the day, in which artificial light showed everything the sun outside could never show. It was the most blissful way of being: all alone in the presence of an intense illusion. Life watched more fascinating than life lived. The other so much more fascinating than the self, a substitute dream for the self. (The eternal bovarysm of the bourgeois boy, satisfied by an industry.)

Because watching is your life. Because you distrust the power over the concrete, which is necessary for life. You experience the film as essential, sublime distance. (And that distance has been removed today. Films inject sensations under your skin, they dump your body across the boundaries of the image, into the image, into the sound. And I think: perhaps that dumping is the new form of distance, a new development in the fundamental cruelty of the film apparatus.)

4.

For the young man, going to the movies was also an answer to art. The boys' game of poetic words and radical slogans did not suit him. The conformism of the literary, formulated "no" surprised him. To him, film was a place to steer clear of all those dubious rules. He chose (indifferent to the censorship of emotions) the shameless brothel of affects. It made him immune to the conflicts between art and commerce, between art and kitsch, between morality and amorality, between conservative film and progressive certainties, between sentimentality and the principle of reality.

Film was definitively a different, radically innocent, free-floating culture, without institutions, without an official language, without norms. It was a low culture, watched with great care by society for its elusive rudderlessness. An uncontrolled territory, a "third world" that anyone with the wildest of imaginations could embark for. A world, too, in which you could stake out an engagement out of no-where, map out your own routes, invent your own genesis and give it ultimate value.

It is true, film lovers have developed their own signaletics, a rudimentary system of traces and smoke signals, in which they only give directions to the initiated. No meetings, no common language, no clauses to which the game could be subjected. Long-journey trekkers never meet. They leave their tracks in such a way that no one could use them for establishing an order. They behave according to a collector's maniacal willfulness.

5.

Dealing with film became a subtle balancing act. It was certainly not enough that they propagated the right conviction, it was not enough that they looked beautiful, it was enough that they felt alive in order to be admired. The criterion was not originality (which happens when film becomes art) but the perceived undeniable rightness with which the images were put on the screen, with which the images set themselves against the world. It didn't matter that others experienced this rightness in places where you didn't. The category is what mattered.

A powerful means of bringing out this rightness was constant re-watching, but also the comparative repositioning of the films, in subtle moves in which qualities became ever more subtly weighted. The smallest distinction contained the biggest difference.

6.

There are films you watch with him, the man, and others you watch with her, the woman.

The film always puts you in a sexualized relationship. In the theater, you forget your own gender, but never gender as such. Images, bodies, and story send you back and forth in that engine that once addressed and "resolved" your sexual identity. The film switches that engine on again and lets the game go its own way, gives you the illusion that the game of chance could have turned out differently. Because in the cinema, you change sex. At least, it is a magic that delights the film lover.

No matter how conformist the stories, role divisions, and prejudices, something radically different happens in the reality of the viewing experience. It is this very conformism that generates in him a shameless travesty. It is conformism that makes these shifts possible, that revolutionizes the viewer. What naivety on the part of those who think they have to emancipate film! It is the very bourgeois clichés that make everything explode.

7.

The watched film is a magic garden for abandoned sons entangled in oedipal impasses—this is what a film lover's profile often looks like. They walk alone in the forest of the seven sons where fathers betray them and others eat them.

Then again, filmmaking is the realm of the father (the dreamed father, the feared stepfather). He shows woman to the sons. The sons look through the father's gaze. The sons discover a form, a style, an attitude, a moral, a possible answer. But the father shows the truly unattainable: the sons have to make do with the image. They are grateful to the father for the view and ask no more, which is why they keep going to the movies. Even when they have long since left the oedipal phase. (How do women like film? Or do they just accompany their friends and men, worried about their restless wandering?)

8.

The fairy-tale belief in photographic images no longer really works. That belief went as follows: because of its photographic basis, film is an undeniable registration. Realistic not because of a stylistic choice, but on the basis of its operation of registering. It is always a technique *of* and *in* the world. The equipment links the film to the world in a radical and astonishing way via a technical umbilical cord.

So watching film and loving film are ways of being with the world. Albeit in a roundabout way that is simultaneously a revelation: a revealing distance. Film is therefore essentially a relationship, not a code. Film is fundamentally the choice of a position in space toward a space.

Film is registration and therefore fundamentally contemporary (one cannot register what is past). The spectator always watches contemporary images (even if they have become old, they remain contemporary as a model). This disposition makes that whoever loves films becomes "contemporary" with every film.

That is why the idea of the classics fails in film: it is a first attempt to install a timeless norm, a law. Film is therefore not only an instrument of distance but also a wondrous way of being with the world. Current affairs are not like that, their theme is not that which is contemporary but that which is out of date. This contemporariness is an instantaneous kind of anthropology that has fueled the awareness of living in one's own world with every fiber of being: the true basis of a political and historical awareness. Or how industrialized dreams fed the consciousness of history as a place of injustice and crime. There is, by the way, a generation that was traumatized into history by that one film by Resnais.[3] With objective registration of the unimaginable, the unthinkable. After that, life has never been the same.

9.

Photographic images are poor. What we see is so familiar that it never overwhelms us. Take, for instance, a shot from Rohmer, Rossellini, or Chaplin: there is so much banal visual noise in their images that they start breathing for that very reason. They have and therefore give space, so that as a spectator you can move, as if the image itself were effectively an open situation. That is why their visual banality acquires an unlimited aspect, like reality itself.

Today's images are being stuffed ever fuller, like a container loaded to the limit. Images chock-full of money, power, cynicism, chock-full of manipulation of meaning, chock-full of ideas too. In the cinemas, these images are now molding the first generation of the second century of film. These images provide an ideal critical education with regard to images. One learns how to treat images in a skeptical, suspicious, even hostile, and contemptuous way, to the delight of the spectator who enjoys being and thinking more than the images he sees. No one in the next century will understand the glorious madness of those who looked up to film. These detached, conscious consumers take up a position that is not a far cry from suspicious moralists.

What challenge could they offer, the images of today luring the spectator, sitting in the brothel window called television? What to do with images that always agree with you, that are there to know and fulfill your desires? What to do in the future after so many images without a future—as there is no money to be made in the future!

10.

A crucial question for those who watch films and want to test their meaning, the world and themselves against it, is the question of the future of that past.

The museum is the institution that gives ready-made and too numerous answers to this question without having listened to the questions. An institution is therefore always something that prevents questions and (new) answers. The museum must simply know what its heritage is, how it should be shown and preserved, and why. The museum is therefore the place of the classics, of authors and of their oeuvre. Nobody seems to believe in it anymore, but it remains.

The academic reflex gives a second answer. It says that films and watching a film are not the core, but that we find ourselves in front of objects that we analyze according to a method to be verified, which often comes at the expense of the film and the film experience itself. Here, one makes room for the typical film, the model film of the film. It is the place of the fragment.

In this context, film is at the mercy of very poor counselors. Those who love film are faced with opponents who are as obstinate as they are embarrassingly insignificant. Once again, one must fight against moralizing readings. Once again it must be said that the film experience is crucial, that this experience is physical-erotic. Once again it must be said that its support is neither celluloid nor magnetic tape but the social self. As simple as it is immensely complicated, the link of each fragmentary "I" to the immense world, of the democratic citizen to the lost whole, has been invaluable to our century. It has made us.

11.

A dream. I gird on the minimum. A sporty outfit to be agile and flexible. I am lowered by a rope into the past, through the narrow hole of an archive. I make my way back through the immense labyrinth of the past hundred years. I leave all maps at home. I start from scratch. I look backward, forward. No longer to write another history, surely—it has been written, it suffices—but to report on experiences. For the very nature of experience is that it is capable of both confirming and questioning everything.

Wasn't life with film above all a life of ever new questions, against the answers of good taste, culture, morality?

IV

Public/Publication/Publishing/Publicity[1]

I distinguish between making photographs and making photographs public. The linking of photography to publicity (as making public) is a social choice, historically situated and subject to change. That linking has a history, it is political in nature (insofar as any publication can be considered a socio-political act).

I take the position that whoever releases a photograph into the public domain can be asked why they do so. I take the position that that justification will determine the manner in which the publication will occur. That manner will play a crucial role in the fate of the photograph and the spectator. This fate will in turn determine the ultimate idea of what photography is, of what publishing means, and of what the public domain contains in terms of possibilities. The question of publishing is ultimately the question of what is to be done in the public domain today.

I wish to assign responsibility to the choice of a photograph and design and to be able to hold it accountable. I demand responsibility for photographs and their publication. I demand a responsible layout; a morality of the picture editor.

In a first set of remarks, I would like to talk about the nature of showing—as the foundation of publishing. I consider that showing as a bodily act and relationship. The responsibility for showing is a bodily approachability: "I" am showing "here," from "my body." Responsibility is not an abstract legal construction but the standing upright of a body that claims itself as a place from which it formulates an answer to the public question. In the system of responsibility, it is the only place from which that answer is possible. In the system of responsibility, it is never "it" (*ça*, the system, culture, the media; or the signifier, power, internal logic) that can answer. The one who shows, bears witness. Today, this has become a position that people want to avoid—people want to avoid a position as such. I will show why that is the case today.

About Showing

For years I would go by every desk in class, holding an opened photo book with both hands, showing the photograph to be discussed. I literally carried the image to the students: I was a *photophore* not a photographer. I realized it was a bit ridiculous, but in the process I learned something essential, namely that showing is actually offering. That it involves a mental, moral, and physical commitment. That it is done with the hands and that the hands offer the image. No, showing images is not a passive, neutral "letting someone see," not an indifferent leaving something lying around. Not only what you show is a weighty decision; how you show is equally weighty. I'll make it even clearer: if you want to cite something to the class, you read it aloud. You let the text pass through your body with your own intonation, interpreting it in a certain way, from a certain relationship. Well, for me, showing images implies a similar embodiment.

Images are nourishment for the eye. They are dishes. A dish is not a pile of foodstuff; it is prepared, arranged, offered, and placed on the plate. People eat via a subtle, all-encompassing rhetoric of offering. That form of giving is contained in the objects that make up the service—it contains the word "to serve." But also the etiquette of serving and receiving is essential to eating.

Mass production and mass consumption of images erode the rhetoric of giving and receiving. The register fundamentally decreases into two caricatures: forced images (forced feeding) and devoured images (compulsive eating). On the one hand, inescapable oversupply, on the other, channel-hopping absorption. Even though these two operations work in opposite directions—feeding versus eating, forced versus willingly, the other who feeds me versus me eating—the two extremes have something essential in common. They are signs of a deranged reception of what is shown. On the one hand, a dismissive "having to look anyway," versus an inattentive "looking past the images."

I—like my generation—am very sensitive to the image that is imposed. Today, the pseudopractice of inattention reigns supreme. Images are a moving mass along which one glides (channel hopping, surfing, grazing, sampling—they form one coherent logic). One superbly escapes constraint but at the expense of the image, which no longer inspires thinking. This practice of distracted viewing is only possible through technology (the remote control as a switch) and through a specific form of distribution (the open channel). It is similar to the light that runs through the cable, is turned on and off, and no longer needs to be made. The image is increasingly "on the channel," with which we have a relationship of switching. With the images themselves, on the other hand, we have a much weaker relationship. One no longer shows us images, they are no longer offered, they are available, merely become retrievable at an ever faster pace. The switch turns a decision into a reflex, a choice into an automatism—the switch removes the weight of commitment and responsibility.

Images increasingly manifest themselves as "unsolicitedly available." The image as epiphany becomes increasingly impossible: the image is always already there—one can neither desire it nor be surprised by it. The demand seems replaced with an ever-larger supply. No exciting scarcity but the impossible choice among excess.

The switch mediates in the choice that has become impossible: simultaneously a choosing for and against, simultaneously choosing and keeping the choice open, never final, always available for instant correction. The switch as a correction key. To make such floating ambivalence possible, one must bypass precisely the body. In the world of objects and gravity, you cannot just let go of the object you are holding, for it will fall. To grasp is to have contact and to commit. To grasp is to engage in the weight and volume of things: the switch spares you that troublesome *physicality*. Showing and receiving an image in a personalized way becomes impossible. There is no more etiquette in our exchange of images. Nor do we even exchange them anymore; we are swimming in the flow they form.

We do not only experience this as our natural everyday reality, it is also an active program, a model of interpretation, a norm. This flow logic settles as an ideal in many practices: the postmodern permanent displacement (its pathetic fear of touch), the loose relationship of text and image (in *Andere Sinema*), the "open" combinations of images among themselves (in *Images/Images*), the undermining of the image as framed and homogeneous by nesting one image in the other and by the erasure of contours (in *Colours*).[2]

It is not a "hot" montage—the exaltation of contrast—but a "cold" collage of the absurd. The nice thing about *Andere Sinema*, for instance, is precisely that slightly hilarious tone that is caused by the selection of images and the typesetting of the title and lead. It is the same laughter we see in publicity for software companies, in the design of MTV, KETNET, and ARTE,[3] of CD-ROMs and websites. It is the smile of comfort, the smile of the switch. They are all sites of postmodern charm design: the charm of irresponsible (i.e., dumb?) irony. Any experience of the image as strange, any shock of the truly unknown is missing. Meaning here must never again be conquered through labor but is jettisoned in the act of consumption. The switch turns off sense.

It is clear to me that the flow and the switching position within it not only discourage and trivialize "sense" but also the possibility of being held accountable. How could one still be reasonably accountable for showing an image if all images are already available anyway, if the system of availability makes any choice unnecessary?

There is a mystique of ubiquity in the New Media and in postmodern reflection on it. One ends up in fantasies of the bodiless, one ignores the point from which one chooses, looks and shows. The umpteenth version of omnipotence, which is always only the umpteenth version of radical powerlessness. It is no accident that the increasing availability of information involves a decrease of the potential to take a stand. Those who are omnipresent can no longer stand against something. Ubiquity is a perspectiveless system of equated observations: enumeration. That is immediately also the principle of the flow.

I do not wish to be complicit in the increasing distraction of my fellow humans. Anyone who claims that it makes them see better is a Pied Piper of Hamelin.[4] Distracted humankind is being fooled entirely—whatever noble pedigree one might derive from Benjamin's cynical point about modernist distraction. In my contact with images, I see less and less where the image comes from, where it wants to take me, I see less and less that it knows and respects itself, that someone longed for that image (and no other) so that it could come into being. Stripped of roots, origin, intention, and strictness toward the one who looks, the image is on the page in a distracted way. Distracted like the anonymous players on the set of a television show: celebrated and yet completely alienated.

Several theses of this century argue that a culture is ultimately the organization of an exchange. Against the gesture of "offering" in showing stands the attitude of "receiving" in looking. Both positions are the basis of every creation narrative, of every social relationship, of every recognition. For me, the elegance with which this complexity is perceived and experienced is at the heart of the showing of images—of what turns the showing into a culture. Distraction, however charming, however sophisticated, is not culture.

But photographs are peculiar images. Their relation to reproduction is quite different from the relation of unique works to reproduction. In photographs, the multiplication is not an external addition to the original shot but is already implicit in the origin. The concept of an image flow, of photography as an environment, is implied in its negative. So there is more to it than just culture and technology choosing multiplication at some point: it was possible because its technical possibility had introduced the concept of multiplication. Besides, the reproduction of other images (of artworks, for instance) does not happen by way of a painted copy but by photographic reproduction. Reproducibility is a photographic project. This is precisely why photographs are not reproduced; they are reproductive as such.

So what can we do with the above plea for responsibility? The inherent reproducibility makes any responsible choice a self-deception: as if you could choose the one drop of salt water from the sea you are swimming in.

Do not photography and all camera images strive to minimize visual responsibility in every way? Is not the camera itself the very switch of visuality? After photography, after the camera, the visual was increasingly thought of as a flow (the unstructured channel) and less and less as the place of the icon (structured meaning).

Is it at all possible to attach a body, an "I," a "here," a justification, a motivation, an attentiveness to such an image type? Or is it only possible—as the postmodernists suggest—to follow and intensify the catastrophic tendency of the thing itself?

In that case, publishing a photograph is a triviality without responsibility (surely photographs are meant to circulate?). If one wants to parry this compelling triviality, one can only do so through the uncomfortable problematization of that tautology (for instance, by saying that nothing deserves the punishment of reproduction; that everything has the right to disappear alone and unique).

The Idiosyncrasy of Photographs

Photographic images do not have an original: the negative is a matrix, not an original; one print is no more original than the other. Reproducibility is the essence of photography: it cannot be defined by its origin.

But in the phase of reproduction, the road between negative and positive is open to a great deal of manipulation. This seems to me to be one of the grounds for a second indefinability of photographs, namely that they can be deployed and offered in all possible contexts. Just as there is no original, so there is no original use. Without an original, there is no standard of proper use either. One can make a photograph public in every conceivable way: the "showing" of photographs cannot target a more correct, more ideal way to do so. No use of a photograph can be interpreted as abuse. There is no benchmark against which the permissibility or impermissibility of a certain use of photographs could be tested. This fosters a brutal, cannibalistic, arbitrary approach to photographs.

Any purism about the right print, about the right use, is based on a phantasm; it is a baseless dream, a fantasy about photography, a desire for an ideal photography (that is, a desire for what is other than photography).

In reality, one can do anything with photographs. That makes them defenseless, weak, but also corrupt. This is precisely why I look for the moralization, the disciplining, the purification of photographs through publication. I do not only want to see the promiscuity of photography but I look for the angle from which they emerge, strict, unapproachable, burning. Even though the spectacle of their festive rearrangements is always fascinating, it remains humiliating to use them as the background of a text, at the service of a New Layout, shamelessly available in image databases. There, they are like smooth pebbles consumed in the flow of use. In that consumption they lose their unruliness, they give up any resistance, smoothed into triumphant trivialities. We wipe our feet on them.

I, for my part, would like to resist this temptation of blatant reuse. Would like to argue in favor of the well-visible, autonomous image unburdened by other images and texts. Would like to argue in favor of a blank field to place it in. Would like to argue in favor of grays and against colorization. Would like to argue in favor of the frame of the negative as the frame of the image. Would like to argue in favor of the illusory hypothesis of the original. This purist view is—who would deny that?—not a neutral but an obsessional one. It imposes on the photograph the unreasonable burden of an autonomy it cannot live up to.

But, at the end of the day, I am after something other than the absolutization of the photograph. I am after the quality of my looking at that image. How do I want to see the photograph? What gesture am I after when showing it? What attitude do I allow my looking to have? What relation to the visual am I after? How much playfulness do I allow myself before it turns into cynicism? How much manipulation can I tolerate before I no longer see the image? To what extent can I bend the image to my will before it becomes a mere projection of my manipulation, before it loses that essential ability of any photograph to resist through its details (through its punctum) my projection, my ideology, my own rhetoric?

Hence my paradoxical proposal, my impossible rule: to show the photograph such that it contradicts, confronts, and challenges me as the one who is showing it—that it turns its back on me. I want to develop strategies that maximize the chances of the image displayed, not my chances as the one who is showing it. To accentuate what is shown *over there*. That means, for instance, keeping a tight rein on all culturalist projects regarding the photograph, and putting them into perspective. No, it is not true that the way a photograph is used is all you can say about it. You should parry any discourse on the photograph by placing the photograph itself in the position of what is resisting it. Against photography as a rhetorical construction of the context, of its publication, I prefer the hypothesis of a context that tries to make the elusiveness of the photograph visible. A context in which a photograph becomes an "appearance" of the truly strange.

At the same time, I realize that every photograph deliberately pursues its own corruption: it is a material that, by nature, seems to bind itself to everything. No threshold whatsoever, no mechanism of rejection of any implantation whatsoever. The image seamlessly adapts itself to any design concept, any classification system, any communication strategy. The photograph betrays every attempt to isolate it, to fix it in its "own" autonomy. But isn't that precisely why its idealization is the ultimate, truly risky challenge?

When asked to comment on contemporary publications of photographs, I replied with a step backward. First by recalling that showing implies a responsibility, a responsibility that is impossible in a flow, where choosing is replaced with being carried, and you are not responsible for that which carries you. Are the New Publications part of the flow or propositions at odds with the flow?

Then I wondered if this responsibility makes any sense in relation to what appear to be images but are in fact something else entirely, namely shots, whose genetic essence is the idea of reproduction. Reproduction is precisely what makes the flow. A flow of choices, of propositions, of originality is contradictory: a choice is always a break, an interruption.

Yet there is a place where both propositions can be, not tested or put into perspective, but put into action. We can, indeed, let the history of publishing act on both propositions. What can we think then?

Mise-en-page

Our century has been defined by two forms of organization: *mise-en-cadre* and *mise-en-page*—in film, the latter is called montage.

In *mise-en-page*, the photographic attitude is effectively given shape. We do not only see photographs on the page but implicitly also a defining relation to photography. As much as we know about the montage, however, as little we know about *mise-en-page*. We have an idea of its importance but we cannot analyze it.

Modernity articulates itself in the union of surface, typography, and photography in a particular combination. But far from everything can be combined. A particular layout requires a particular image, namely a specific *mise-en-cadre*. The style of one must be compatible with that of the other. Just as a particular film frame includes a particular montage and excludes another, so there is a stylistic combination between the photo frame and layout. This unsurprising observation does, however, contradict my second thesis, which says that photographs can be used and reused without limit.

One could go even further and establish a connection between a particular quality of what is photographed (a building in a particular style, a particular vision of the architectural) and a particular way of placing it in the frame. Subject, *mise-en-cadre* and *mise-en-page* carry on through as a stylistic continuum. And the *mise-en-page* might play a very important role in that. It is the scale in which the framed image has been fitted, in which, in turn, the motif is embedded. The *mise-en-page* as a practical territory in which major choices are made with regard to photography and photographed reality, and on which responsibility is centered, eventually.

The question of how to make photographs public begins with answering the questions "why" and therefore "how" you want to give them "what kind" of visibility. That question is answered in the concrete terms of pages, of the way they are filled and their organization. It is a paper stage on which usually a text is played that no one knows, that is directed by no one, and whose instruments never get attuned to one another, so that a photographic *mise-en-page* invariably resembles the cacophony of a tuning orchestra. It is not surprising that one likes to escape this by forcing the photographs in line—they always say something but it is never synchronized. One always wants to make photographs speak because they are so ear-splittingly silent. I love it when photographs can make their silence heard.

The Blurred Photograph: An Old Debate[1]

First there is blur, then comes the one correct sharpness. First matter, then form, the word (and there is only one correct word). In the jungle of countless blurs, the unique sharpness is an improbable miracle.

Focusing comes after the choice of a motif. First you see the subject with the naked eye, then you look at it through the device: through a frame but also through a lens that you must focus. Focusing is an aspect of good observation: the oriented and precise knowing what you want to see and show. But also what you don't want to show. What you don't want to show, is hard to remove from your image; so you try not to emphasize it, you push it back through blur. Focusing on one motif means blurring other motifs. The frame delineates an even field; within that field, the focusing indicates, chooses, aims, orients, accentuates. The focusing uses the sharp point to show what you have to see. It decides, it determines. It says: that and not the other.

Onscherpte is the Dutch word for "unsharpness" or "blur." It is composed of *scherpte* [sharpness] and the prefix of negation *on-* [un-]. The language immediately steers the debate; the construction of the word forces sharpness to be placed first (as opposed to the concrete photographic experience). But since there is only the one rare correct sharpness, it is automatically valued positively. In French, blur is called *flou*; a neutral word, even though the meaning is more often negative than positive here as well.

In Dutch, the very terms "sharpness" and "unsharpness" explain the link between both. They are two poles of one category (says the semiotician). "Sharpness" and "unsharpness" are thus neither absolute nor isolated but rather relative and linked values. "Sharp" is in a permanent dialogue with "unsharp" and vice versa. Separately, they lose their meaning, becoming a characteristic that is no longer pertinent (says the semiotician). Precisely because of their polarity, one can use both in the creation of an image. "Unsharpness" contrasts with something we perceive as "sharper" and, conversely, "sharpness" is only that which is "less unsharp." Sharp and unsharp have no absolute measure [in Dutch]. It is a sliding impression of more or less with regard to a contrasting zone.

Blurred is an optical impression that a print gives you. That impression relates to two aspects: the figures that can be seen in the image ("Is it sharp?") and the quality of the image surface. Blur not only shows figures in a certain (less detailed) way but also suggests the existence of a photographic matter. The image that is blurred not only contains information about the figures but also makes tactile suggestions: the blurred is soft, woolly, more material. It seems as if the photographic non-matter acquires substance after all, and becomes a tangible medium. In sharp images, on the other hand, that matter seems always to disappear into its informative function. The more information (details), the less matter and, conversely, the less information, the more the details of the medium come up.

"Unsharpness" is a sensory impression that has a technical basis. For many, an image that is blurred is a technically poorly made image: wrong shutter speed, bad focusing. Blur immediately attracts a technical discussion (how come it is blurred?), smuggling in technical standards. The technique itself prescribes the correct, optimally sharp image as its ideal use. There is a correct way of using the equipment and an incorrect way!

But even if one reverses the values and (as often happened in photography) chooses blur as a positive category (against the all too literal sharpness), then, if anything, blur is even more considered to be a technique. Blur is most certainly a technically determined characteristic of the image, but it is also an optical impression on the side of the spectator. One does not explain this impression on the side of the observer by referring to the technique. The technique can offer no useful argument in weighing the respective values of sharpness and blur. The correct technical use is one thing, the aesthetically meaningful application is quite another. In photography, the technique must constantly be put in its proper place: it warrants a result, agreed, but the appreciation of this result cannot be a technical affair!

Hence the fact that blur is approached here only as the effect an image has on the spectator. Sharpness and blur structure the image for the observer; they steer the interpretation of the image, and we are precisely concerned with how that happens. How does the spectator experience blur (in its many variants)? What kinds of images are produced by these different kinds of blur? The answer to the question of how blur was created technically guides our reading but it does not describe its effects qua meaning and sensory perception. That is why I call sharpness and blur technique-effects. We do not see a technique, we see its image effect; we know that technique, not craft, is its basis, but we are not looking at a technical preparation; we are looking at an image imaginatively. That effect brings us to that very specific "craft" of the beholder.

With the expression *le fini*, nineteenth-century art practice and theory raised a problem of sharpness. It was about perfect detail, about getting rid of the material traces of paint and the application of paint, about the perfect, transparent, figurative legibility of every zone of the image. Innovative painters and critics rebelled against this. They opted to leave the material and the act of painting visible in the final result. This meant that the power of improvisation and spontaneity, typical of the sketch, would become part of the register of finished work.

A very different situation arises with the blur of photography. Photographic blur (the painterly "non-finito") has nothing at all to do with improvisation and quick sketching; it is a deliberate addition afterward. Pictorialism does not yield a spontaneous photograph but a photograph with a supplement; not direct impression but the laborious manipulation of it afterward. This manipulation may produce a vague result, but the vagueness has nothing to do with improvised unfinishedness. The vagueness is not original but added. In photography, the blur looks academic and artificial, not lively and improvised: the blur becomes photography's very own *fini*.

There are different sorts of blur, each the result of a different technical operation with very specific effects for the image and its interpretation. The above remarks dealt with the entire image being blurred, which was obtained in the darkroom and/or by the choice of the paper. However, this is not the only form of blur. There is also motion blur or "incorrect" focusing. In each case, this involves a different type of blur, a different strategic placement of it in the image.

There is all-over blur of the entire image surface and local, partial blur. Motion and focal blur are usually localized; grain and darkroom manipulations usually result in all-surface blur. But even this is not a law. Movement and focusing are aspects of taking photographs, while the choice and handling of the paper belong in a different category.

Playing with local blur through movement or focusing gives the images a reportage feel. Global blur, on the other hand, pushes the photograph out of the register of the snapshot and gives it a slow, considered, more "plastic" character.

The various "techniques" tend toward these effects but do not necessarily lead to them; they can be combined and generate new nuances each time. Take Sanne Sannes's photography: a combination of grain blur, focal blur, and motion blur, leading to a blurring of the whole image without detracting from the dynamics of the images, which is very unpictorialist indeed.

But what happens with *local* blur? A sharp and a blurred area appear in one image. Their contrast is striking and active. The contrast indicates a deliberately employed distinction between what you want to show properly and what you don't want to show. It indicates a point of view and a choice: you were there, at that moment, and you were looking at that but you also allowed that (blurred) thing to happen in your image. The local blur points to the shot and reveals the photographer, his act and choice. The photographer actively and compellingly steers the interpretation of the image away from the blurred (from what is present but unimportant, because it is undefined) to the sharp part. There, the photographer points out: that is my subject.

On the other hand, there is the all-over sharpness or blur. No contrast within the image (but with other images), since the entire image surface obeys one and the same effect. These are therefore two "simple" forms, which represent two fundamentally different choices regarding photography. The all-over sharpness chooses maximum precision and visibility. A maximum depth of field in which the whole space and *all* details are available *at once*. An obscene revelation of everything in its boldest visibility. An objectifying indifference, since everything is equated. The technique par excellence of neutral information, of descriptive photography: inventory and identification. All-over sharpness excludes choices in the image. The photograph demands from its spectator the courage of cold-blooded apathy (no sympathy, no antipathy, but neutrality). This photography implicitly says: the image result draws its strength from the radically neutral way in which it came into being. (One often identifies that neutrality with objectivity. Isn't that bland, objectivity obtained through being neutral? Aren't objectivity and neutrality fundamentally opposing notions?)

The pictorialist photographer (of the all-over blur) says that the means of photography are all indiscriminately at your disposal to achieve a beautiful result in whichever way. Don't ask how, look at the result! The photography of sharpness says: don't look at the result, ask how it was done.

The all-over blur first of all veils the details, drastically reducing their number. It thwarts a clear reading of volumes and space. Not through a mist in the motif, but through a layer that is separate from the motif and is added elsewhere afterward. At that moment, photographic matter itself comes to the fore, at the expense of the differentiated representation of the motif. Against the glassy aquarium effect of sharpness now stands the tactility of the paper and its grain. Whereas sharpness lifts the motif from the paper (dripping like a corpse lifted out of the water), blur lets the motif go under in the paper (like a person drowning in water). This is neither a choice for neutral information (the sharp image) nor for engagement in the space of what is represented (as with focal blur) but against information, against space and for an engagement with matter.

The idea of motion blur is a late addition to the photographic lexicon. Until deep into our century, time was of no use to photography. To photograph was to fixate, but it assumed that the subject itself was already fixated. Sharpness fixated and denied the moment, that explosive fraction of the shot. Motion blur, on the other hand, captures motion itself in a trace. Motion blur typically turns a photograph into a failed image. After all, blurring makes the motif appear in the image in a lesser way. It requires a deliberate decision to recognize that lesser presence, that disappearing appearance as photographically significant.

Motion blur is not poeticizing, like all-over blur, but dynamizing and plastic. The figure "sweeps" vaguely across the image. It disappears, sometimes literally becoming translucent. The figure withdraws from the three-dimensional space in which it moved and tilts into its two-dimensional negation. At the same time, the evidence that something happened in time slides into the fixated image, something that makes the just-before and just-after of the closing shutter visible. The moving body is cut (hit) by the cut in time and, very briefly, mortally wounded, bleeding and screaming in the image (a horror effect).

In this way, space and time, as torn apart in photography, merge for a moment. A movement in time-space leaves a trace in a plane. The movement itself disappears in that trace, detaching itself from what is moving and becomes visible as the ultimate abstraction: pure movement. Here, time conceals and movement masks, instead of divulging, expressing, revealing. Surely everywhere else, movement is the ultimate proof of the presence of strength, energy, vitality. In photography, movement is the beginning of disappearance. Here, movement does not affirm the moving but ignores it to the benefit of itself, of movement.

The local motion blur is (not coincidentally) a nonanalog formation of the image (it does not resemble what is depicted), its abstract index. The "sharp" photograph, on the other hand, effortlessly reconciles the analog and the index character in the photograph. Motion blur is an index sign that only exists in photography: nowhere else in observable reality does motion blur occur. No movement in reality we see as motion blur. Movement is always linked to something that moves.

Even though motion blur and focus often occur in the same type of images, the two are very different. Focus modulates the perception of something in space; motion blur projects an object-in-time from space onto a plane. Focal blur is simple and, along with all-over blur, easily recognized as a perceptual defect. Motion blur is something else entirely.

Sharpness and blur have been judged very differently throughout the history of photography. Every debate on this subject is a fundamental debate on photography; it diametrically opposes contrasting views on the essence of photography. It is definitely more than a subjective difference in taste. Nothing less than the soul of the medium is at stake.

In photography, precision is really too precise, the many details too much: the abundance of information creates a lack of clarity, incoherence; because of the excess, the image loses order, legibility, sense. It acquires a chaotic and brutal character, the details canceling out each other or even the whole thing. The image becomes inhuman through detail. It becomes part, as Henri Van Lier would say, of *le réel* [the real] and is no longer child of *la réalité* [reality]. Roland Barthes uses punctum to indicate what is essentially photographic for him, namely the unique ability to make possible, in any arbitrary point (unplannable by either photographer or spectator), a brutal irruption of facticity into the status of the image.

Against this, blur (both its all-over and darkroom version) is not the mastery of details (as it sometimes claims) but—more radically—the destruction of the photographic surface. Mutilation rather than simplification, a wound rather than abstraction. And all that of an image, the photograph, that is pure surface! The image does not become more accessible, more comprehensible, and simpler now that it has been stripped of that inexhaustible amount of detail; quite the contrary, the image now becomes definitively blurred. It loses that unique photographic power that lies in the all too real collision of light, object, and celluloid. In the case of blur, the object leaves the photographic surface, withdraws, steps out of the image, and acquires a spectral quality. The all-over blur creates a (pseudo) depth behind the surface into which it hazily withdraws. Of course, this artistic-looking form of blur seeks the depth that is so characteristic of the classic arts that really work with matter. But photography is an art without matter, and the suggestion of depth creates an illusion at the price of a very real mutilation.

Does the photographer write with light? Doubts about that are growing again. A photograph is said to be an image like any other: a medium filled with planes and traces. The new blur does not grow out of the old image ideal (as was still the case with the pictorialists). In fact, it grows against all forms of local blur (which only poses the reality question at the expense of the image question). The new blur has to do with skepticism, with blindness—it is not homage to and exaltation of looking but its negation. Looking is sin and hubris, groping is good. Let us make tangible images and ideas.

In closing. Sharpness is an ideal, not only in photography; it is a malefactor, not only in photography. Sharpness is at stake in a fundamental and ultimately unfounded choice. This writer loves sharpness: in images, in thought, in language. To try to capture complexity with a blur is a mere tautology. Besides, complexity is not blurred; vagueness and simplification go together. Sharpness is the endless task of showing (and not just undergoing) complexity, of facing the unintelligible supremacy not with laziness or demagoguery but in a snappy and sharp manner. The sharp person opts for the fight, or at least for opposition. Vagueness always echoes the acceptance of supremacy; sharpness says "no."

The Image That Yields Up Everything (Because It Has Seen Nothing)[1]

Warning/Rules of the Game

This is not a commentary on Benjamin but on photography. Now, that is not something you claim lightly; hasn't every commentary on photography since 1931[2] been a footnote to those few pages by Benjamin?

But what exactly did Benjamin know about photography? What images were part of his familiar environment: what were the books he bought, the periodicals that filled the newsstands of the time, the daily practice of private photographing? What did he know about being photographed, about looking at photographs, about photography as illustration, as document and advertisement?

The period in which he developed his ideas about photography is one of the richest in the history of the photographic image. The spectator realizes this afterward, when he can look back over the many experiments. But not everything was as visible at the time. Did Benjamin know the work of Brassaï, Cartier-Bresson, Kertész? And importantly, how did he know it? As what? Through what interpretation?

To be clarified, too, is the theme of this essay: is it about a style, namely "surrealist photography" (in the version of Krauss and Livingston), or is it on the contrary about photography in general, which is considered as fundamentally surrealist (in the version of Sontag)?[3]

Meanwhile, the role of photography has become quite different today. The power of photography today has to do with its "becoming image." Photography is growing away from document, registration, and representation as "automatic truth." It is losing its status of epistemic magic. It is at the service of mechanisms that were not even concepts at the time: communication, information, media. All phenomena that Benjamin points to but which were not yet the obvious horizon of knowledge of all society. Benjamin discovers that these optical devices are social devices, social models, but society itself is not yet aware of its own creeping transformation. That photography has acquired artistic prestige today goes against his warnings. But perhaps this misplaced assessment gave photography a very strategic position.

The Anonymous Image

Surrealism intervenes in photography in a reflective way: its weaknesses, unusual procedures, surprising possibilities, and peculiar consequences are perceived, valorized and often formulated in powerful visual ideas. They manage to name and think about the radical novelty of this kind of image—because the surrealists' starting point allows them to evaluate those peculiarities positively. Indeed, their starting point is photography, from which they set up a peculiarly unpredictable game of values.

The surrealist starting point is art without artists, nameless architecture, ethnographic objects, vernacular utensils, artisanal traditions, and most certainly also those very new images made by machines. All this forms an endless line of *traces*, along with a genuine interest in the visual forms of whatever origin: generous tolerance and openness to values and forms. But at the same time, it is also a provocative inversion, a perverse inversion, a pseudo-naive ignorance of the "normal" relations between useful and beautiful, artistic sensibility and art history, creation and creativity, image and imagination. This strategy of confusion has been so successful that it resulted in a permanent ban on the expression of values.

Camera images fit into this strategy of considering images as *traces*. In the case of an "artwork," one does not speak of a trace: the artwork clearly reveals its origin and intention. One speaks of a trace when the intention and origin are unclear because they were not brought up. The object described as a trace is at once the antipode of the artwork. The trace is impersonal because it came into being (not: was made) as an "aside," an unintended side effect on the margins of another, central activity. As the trace has no "author," it automatically belongs to the public domain: anyone can take, freely interpret, and endlessly rearrange it. A trace is not claimed by anyone, so anyone can appropriate it with impunity.

Photography is registration: a trace of light. Only two factors are of importance during the actual shot: energy and chemical matter. Every photograph is a kind of trace of fire, which is made clear by the blackening of the material. This has tremendous consequences for the intentional structure of the image and its interpretation: a photograph is an "image of what is photographed" not of the photographer.

As light influences the shot autonomously, unforeseeable combinations, accidents, unplannable "facts" creep into the photograph object. The celluloid as the site par excellence of the *anonymous encounter*: unintended and unsought.

Another point: precisely this automatic nature of the exposure functions as the overall program for the entire apparatus. The automatic nature of the shot as the core of the process is extended to all aspects of photographing: the device is "fully automatic." "Anyone" can take pictures with it, because all functions have been automated: that is the message to promote the industry and the medium.

This creates an enormous stream of images, which on the one hand are very private and on the other hand radically disappear into anonymous stereotypy. It is automatic devices that make the images, according to the preprogrammed plan of the industry. Every photograph is the "work" of that technical-industrial program. But every photograph is also the trace of something else, which cannot be captured in image formulas and be neutralized by programs. The intriguing thing about photography is the strange relationship of the industry's anonymous authorship and the unconscious presence of a unique trace as both a perverse indication and denial of a unique moment, a concrete place and an individual maker.

A final thought concerning the trace: photography is the found object par excellence. There are enormous archives everywhere, temporary gatherings, stalls of photographs sticking together—like fish stalls— from which any random selection may turn out to be a miraculous catch. It is not the images themselves, but the gaze of the strolling fisherman-passer-by that is creative. His sensitivity determines whether something from that jumble will float to the surface, be chosen and through that choice be given a new chance of survival.

"Surrealist photography"—the adjective in that expression does not play a specifying but a defining role. All photography is potentially surrealist. Especially photography that does not present itself as surrealist. (Just as Atget did not want his name linked to the surrealist style. The very "stylelessness" of his images makes them irresistible—naive and inexhaustibly suggestive—to the surrealist eye). No, surrealist photography is the image that has always already been made. The image is always there before the awareness of it, separate from that awareness. A photograph is that which is given, not that which is made; that which can be reacted to, not that which is directed, humanized. It is a thing-image that happens to float by. And only then does the surrealist moment dawn: in the ability to ignite an image that is "unaware" of its emotional fuel.

No "Critical" Image

Curiously, surrealism is precisely not a sociological, mass-media reading of the (photographic) image. Its inversions have nothing to do with social codes and values that one subjects to criticism (as, for instance, Barthes and Eco do), but with modes and orders of experience.

There is a spectral character to images and to what is depicted. "Ghosts," not codes, are living in the images that the surrealists make of cities, streets, interiors, and bodies.

It is the ultimate offshoot of esoteric sensibility, were it not that any submission to the authority of what is thus revealed is alien to them. They seize what is revealed with sensual glances and hands. They touch and eroticize it. They fill it with matter and concreteness: it is the matter that is mysterious, not what is behind or above it. Hence the fact that photography is a rewarding instrument for this strategy of attention and reading. Not a spiritualistic magic trick suggested through double exposures but the most banal visibility filling itself with the unspoken.

The Blind Image

Photography is based on modern technology and in spite of this (or because of it?) only produces remains. Photography is fundamentally a mechanism of disposal: it is never events, phenomena, or persons that appear here but only traces of them. The image parasitizes the "actual" and the "original," and does not meet with the appreciation an original work would meet with.

Photographs are the remains of everyday life, the inversion, the negative of visible, explicit, everyday existence. It is the trivial, routine, and machine-like other side in the shadow of social and individual life. Just as the social is the nocturnal other side of one's own individual experience of life, namely the humiliating correction to the curious sense of being "oneself." Just as that sense of individuality is belied by a social interpretation, so the sense of life is belied by photography.

Photographs: remainder, waste, dump. A curious neoprimitive material in which the hidden codes, the implicit regularities of modern life are fixed. Photography is instant ethnographic material: at once the expression and documentation of existence without history, of the permanent structures beneath the surface, of the anonymity that determines all utterances (something Atget was apparently well aware of). In this sense, photography is a trace that is all the more revealing because it is unconscious, and as a trace it is the great denier of all forms.

What stands out is the radical *apathy* of these "utterances," which are actually documents. The cruel and obscene are recorded without any emotional reaction, without recognition of what is to be seen, of what shows itself in the image. In unmoved objectivity, in an unblinking law of light and perspective, photography captures *everything*. Photography is a model and school of something much more radical than neutrality and objectivity, namely indifference. There is an attention to detail here that is possible only through inattention (because there is no recognition, no linguistic identification). A photograph never shows that it recognizes something: it shows that it recognizes *nothing*. Photography registers, but it does not see anything. As a mere optical device, it is the negation of looking. The photograph that reveals so much, that reveals everything, has never seen anything itself.

What makes photography so powerful and irresistible emotionally is precisely that all-important ground of a-emotionality. What makes photography a model of (the so highly valued) objective knowledge is its unique ability precisely not to know anything at all. (Is not the photograph the archetype of our information, the preeminent way of not knowing, may I say: negating?) The photograph is the document that reveals by shirking all cognitive categories and rules.

In every photograph, we painfully experience how we as spectators, unlike the device, are the prisoners of our pathetic mode of existence, of our capacity for registering and at the same time of our radical and fatal boundedness in language and identity.

The photographic "ascopia" can be interpreted as both naive and perverse. Hence the fact that sentimentality and perversity have both found their way into photography. Photography also makes clear that both of these relationships, as opposites, have a lot in common. Kitsch and camp find photography to be an ideal breeding ground. For that matter, there is a substantial premium for "bad taste" in photography.

Conscious, aesthetic photography is blind to these fundamentals. It controls the device when shooting, it controls the image when developing and printing, it imposes a direction, it organizes its interpretation, binds the image to a form through text, captions and image combinations. Art photography seeks to undo the primary ascopia and apathy: the camera sees and reveals—and how! The surrealist approach to photography suggests something else entirely, namely that one should not bend its private essence but undergo it.

Technically speaking, surrealist shots are rather "primitive," although all sorts of pseudosurrealisms invest mainly in "effects." But technical manipulations are precisely means of control over the image, deliberate intervention in and bending of automatism. They try to give visual indications of interpretation to that which goes by without indication. All these interventions are as many rebuttals of what is so fascinating about the medium.

Surrealist photography is at its weakest when it has a conscious, intended character; when its possibilities become a theme of an explicit program. Surrealist photographs are strongest when they loosely, carelessly, haughtily evade any project, any style or theme: when they try to escape the externalities of the oeuvre. It is only when one pretends that none of it matters that the image can reveal an awakening of secret forces: in things, in the allegorical speech of time, in the rhythms and especially the wounds of time.

It is the "visual speechlessness," the visual illiteracy of anonymous photography that fundamentally shows the surrealist effectiveness of the image type. Because of the maker's limited control over the image, because of the lack of a clear desire to control the image, all kinds of slips nestle in the image. By registering what one has not seen, visual consciousness exercises no control and therefore no censorship. It is as if, for a moment, the "libido of things" is visually caught in a rear-view mirror: their secret soul life, their tragedy of impermanence and usefulness, their temporary triumphs and their necessary decay and eventual lostness, which one often sees in cities and in the cycle of consumption. All this is made openly visible for the first time through photography. And this truth about things turns out to apply to people as well.

The photograph as an object obviously takes part in this, too. It is extremely impermanent; a machine product, incorporated into a triumphant cycle of endless reproducibility, which makes its very survival much less likely.

Achronia

There is no crucial moment in surrealist photography, no temporal climax, no "decisive moment" (Cartier-Bresson) in which something culminates into a clear form. Photography is the preeminent means of showing achronia, just as it has atopia as its "territory." Photography de-dramatizes time, stripping it of its narrative arc and dropping the image into a radical *hors-temps.* Not surprising, then, that there is so much speculation about the time of photography in order to ward off that achronia with all sorts of constructions.

But the photograph precisely does not make present (Barthes concealed that point[4]). On the contrary, the photograph leaves radically indifferent and therefore it has no time. Barthes underscores the temporal pathos of photography, and thereby does away with the notion that the photograph relies on apathy as the most fundamental experience of the camera image. What Barthes describes is a very familiar felt experience of the photographic; but to do so, he needs to suppress the radically other experience, which is all the more concealed because it is so much more common but also so much more incomprehensible.

About Monuments

The subject of surrealism is the monument. A time machine par excellence. Social par excellence. Coded par excellence.

It continues the history of nineteenth-century photography, which was primarily a debate with the monumental. That was at the same time its subject, which also determined its specific imagery. As a view on the monument, photography discovered its first forms: frontal, symmetrical, and orderly. As a view on the modernist monument, the new photography (*Das Neue Sehen*) developed very different image forms: fragmentation, diagonal, side, bottom, and top views.

With arms crossed and legs out, the nineteenth-century monumental photograph stands triumphantly against the world—which always appears in the image as a kind of monument. Thus stand the heroes on the stage of the melodrama, in the early scenes of feuilletons, in the photographs from the colonies, and in the workshop. These photographs shamelessly claim reality in its most grandiose expression: nature, big game, and architecture.

For the surrealist, this triumphant attitude is mostly comical and enigmatic. The surrealist does not put the monument into perspective, he handles it. The purport (in the images of Brassaï and Boiffard, with

Atget as inspiration) is not disconcerting, but reenchanting. The monumental is composed in the key of the enchanting, the comic, and the obscene.

The monumental is a grammatical mode, a key peculiar to objects, texts, and images, but it is also a mode of behavior, utterance, and watching. The surrealists constantly employ a monumentalizing visual form in the face of banal, everyday reality. The monumental is used in a misguided way. It can be linked to the biological, to decay, and to residual functions. The trace, which is fundamentally unmonumental, is monumentalized.

The historical rhetoric of the monumental is an ideal mode for surrealist operations. Rhetoric is the illusionary game par excellence; historicity is both a product of that rhetoric and instantaneously invalidated by that very rhetoric. Not criticism but aberrant application.

The Matter of Time

The monument is the place of death. The monument has to do with memory: it is linked to the position of photography itself and its souvenir nature. Every photograph is a tombstone, a gravestone, a construction that pays tribute in a cold, official, routine way. Every photograph is a ritual of commemoration with a parade, poses, centralizations, a shuffling gait, and suppressed liveliness. Just as each monument makes visible the ultimate petrification, the photograph brings petrification within everyone's reach, turns it into a daily performable ritual act. Photography is a machine for the automated production of monuments, for the instantaneous performance of a commemoration. In that case, says the surrealist sensibility, photography has nothing to do with passing but is the very antipode of the snapshot, has no part in any fundamental way in the cult of the vivid, spontaneous image that, in the early reportage photography of the same period becomes the essence of twentieth-century photography.

Against these images, the surrealist interpretation says photography sculpts time rather than undergoing it; dominates time rather than swimming in it; immobilizes time into one great mass of ice rather than following the elusive frolicking of the instant.

In time as volume, as body, as space and extensiveness, different fragments of time can float across the image like lumps of *temporal matter*. The photograph suddenly becomes a razor-thin interface where divergent temporal orders and forms slide past each other. In that "touching" of each other, neither the instant nor pastness takes place, but another, peculiar experience of time: a lightening, a vague projection, a suggestion, a virtual configuration. Never undeniably evident but always of the order of doubt. Is what one thinks one sees suggestion and illusion, or evidence?

The surrealist position regards the evidential value of the photograph as a marginal feature: it is not that kind of "truth" it values. For surrealism, the evidential value praised by all realist readings of photography (but are there others?) is a triviality compared to other, much more peculiar possibilities.

The Dull Dialogue

The photograph is essentially made "between" a model and a photographer; every photograph is a moment from a dialogue, was first an image that went back and forth between a photographer and a subject, between watching and showing. The photograph closes around that into a closed circuit in which all the terms of the event are present in the image itself. In this sense, a "successful" photograph is a document of a live encounter.

Surrealism explores what happens when that "between" does not take place, when the lively back and forth becomes blocked. That automatically causes the typical dullness of too emphatically, too frenetically posed images.

The photography they prefer has been cut in half. What is missing is the phase of giving/accepting the image, the moment when the image is offered and received. The arrival of the image here is not joyful but misunderstood and incomprehensible—a source of a dull panic, of a dumb expressionlessness, a moment of the most banal and therefore perhaps the most obscene getting caught. A moment when the human gaze in the camera and the human gaze *through* the camera have not formed a "figure." They reveal themselves as an incoherent collection, a bizarre collage, an amalgamation.

An image of the studio, of the world, of humankind *as a workshop*. Yet, there is no smith, no creator to be discerned in these images: it is clearly the seventh day, the day of rest, the day of the ultimate lostness of things, the day of a petrified, humorless, tensionless carnival in which nothing is itself anymore, or rather, in which everything is limited to its own contours in the most fatal of ways.

The Panic Monologue

In a sense, every shot reduces all relationships to monologues, all confessions to self-confessions, all seduction to narcissism. In a photograph, things may look in the direction of the camera inquiringly, but ultimately they are mostly looking at themselves like in a mirror. They are looking for their own image over there. The photographer, too, looks through his viewfinder at "that" image over there, as if looking at an image that will reveal *him*. Finally, the spectator, too, looks at each photograph as if at a reflecting surface. They all experience the photograph as something that suddenly freezes, fossilizes, and immediately loses its reflecting character. A frozen and thus blind mirror.

Everyone and everything is caught up in a peculiar kind of self-reflection; that is the surrealist signature. Every photograph is the image of expectation. That expectation is unfocused, not exuberant, yet there is a vague projective relationship. Even the spectator of the image beholds a magic mirror in which everything is *en attente* [waiting] for a movement, a salvation, and an awakening, a finally, finally becoming "real" again (unreal the photograph, the photographer, the photographed, the one who allows himself to be caught in the photograph).

The image shows how the world waiting over there slowly but also inescapably slips away into a delusion: the delusion of being oneself in a future time. Of being "now" as the one who (a)waits. Barthes writes that photography shows something "now" that is irrevocably past; but the delusion of time applies in the other direction as well: to show something "now" that one will be. Benjamin named that effect in relation to the portrait of Dauthendey.[5] He constructed a breathtaking sentence structure around it to capture the windings of time in one phrase.

If everything in photography is of the order of waiting—being there, but focusing on what is not there yet (and never will be)—then the following conclusion about the essence of the photographic could perhaps be formulated: it is preeminently an image without a figure. If we understand "figure" in its etymological sense, namely as an *activity* in which a *form* (figure, as one says "having a nice figure") is given to unformed matter, then we see that photography can never make a figure.

Essentially, photography is "afigurative"—which means *defiguring*. What fascinated the surrealists about photography is its ability to make an image, a depiction, a correct representation, and to do so precisely by way of mutilation. The photograph makes visible and punishes the visible, branding that which shows itself in its most blatant zone, namely in the face (of people, things, landscapes). A face that becomes object and abject, an image of sex, rather than of exalted interiority. Things, too, are given a face and are thus imposed a gender in an ambiguity that wants to be hurtful and shameful, rather than obscene and defiant.

The centrality and frontality of the image, of the face in the image, of the eye in the face, is broken here. One can only look at these photographs from a broken, sideways, adverse angle. What the photograph shows is reality as mutilation.

V

Moving House[1]

"I'd rather not write about contemporary art anymore," goes my urgent request. Later, the question, "Why that rejection?"

Yes, why? Why does one move house? And above all how? Where to? How does one lose interest? How does one rationalize that loss? How does one turn that loss into gain (namely, liberation)?

As soon as I deal with contemporary art—that specific form of art that wants to be contemporary, that, urgently, needs a place here and now, I whiff an all-consuming, insufferable *mauvaise conscience*.

In art, all participants are agnostics but still perform the ritual. It is the same perfume with which politicians jokingly sell a new politics, managers a new corporate culture. Nothing has substance, everything is mere label. Salesmanship is everything and that is the place for the new intellectuals: traders in false arguments.

No one is duped; there is just no place for the unsuspecting victim of these tricks. Even though I would gladly take the victimhood and keep the innocence, it is no longer available. The impossibility of sincerity has become unlivable to me. The pedagogy that helped us grow away from the simplicity of naivete, toward mature originality, has been replaced with a diner for take-home cynicism. The art world as a hamburger joint for ceaseless relativism.

The artists' despair and cynicism are no longer tolerable. Their social unhappiness is bottomless. It is necessary to protect oneself from it.

The bad conscience of contemporary art manifests itself in the desperate absence of enthusiasm.

The bad conscience manifests itself in resentment; it is the envy, the sorrow of unrequited love. As in Koolhaas's reprehensible Kunsthal in Rotterdam[2]—every visitor is a sap, so wake him up with a crooked floor; insult him by squeezing him into a ludicrous entrance; render him so unsure of his competence that he goes down on his knees and asks, "Where is it? What is it?"

Bad conscience manifests itself in the way art wants the visitor to perform the labor of art. Nothing seems more natural today than projects in which one challenges the visitor, throws questions at him, enforces awareness from him! That intolerable interference, that youth-camp drill, that vulgarity with which one wants to challenge, touch, and manipulate me. Art does not "place" me anywhere, no, it expects from me the answers to its unresolved questions. The visitor as artist, indeed, as raison d'être of the artwork! I am a visitor precisely in order not to be an artist! I look for a raison d'être in art!

The reopening of the Centre Pompidou—the exhibition *Le temps, vite*.[3] Objects that count as art are set up in an amusement park, in a game-like trajectory with codes and keys, with commands and insufferable veils that suggest false discretion, as if I were going through a very indiscreet experience. A miniature repetition of Lyotard's scandalous *Les Immatériaux*.[4] The impression that I am nothing but a chunk—not biological but mental matter. One wants *bio-pouvoir* over that biological life and attention power over my mental life. After the scientific organization of the movements of labor, the control and organization of mental movements. The museum of the contemporary is a testing ground. A factory hall for the information energy released by the mental.

The museum is always one of the faces of ruling power. Today museums show contemporary art, art as actuality. Power no longer operates through history but exclusively as actuality.

The actuality of art generates a specific form of intellectuality: the in-ability to simply call things by their names. That inability reduces all thinking to speculation. Thinking is different from speculating. In speculation, thinking plays, gambles, amuses itself—speculation knows no bounds, is sophistic, speculation is "thinking through" beyond the ground under its feet. One thinks beyond what is there, as a limit but also as a task. Thinking is so much more laborious because it thinks through, along with, by means of something else. That slow compromise with the other makes up the difficulty and value of thinking. Speculation, on the other hand, is thinking about that which did not make you to think. What makes you to think, makes you shut up in the first place. What doesn't make you think, makes you babble.

The postmodern is a license for speculative thinking. The young Sartre was delighted by the fact that you could philosophize about any-thing, especially about the most mundane things; today one is delighted because one can respond to essential questions in whatever way. A shift from the triumph of the trivial subject to the triumph of the trivialized method. No commitment to a way of thinking but a grotesque sampling of ways and styles of thinking. Mental kitsch.

The museum architecture is the ideological program for the visitor—the instruction manual. The Centre Pompidou has longer lines than ever and the counter counting visitors is still there. Each visitor allows him-self to be counted, submits to the numbers, sees his entire role reduced to that function. I was marked no. 1472.

The Centre's controversial city cycle was the spectacular gong-stroke of a new relationship. Sociological completeness had sabotaged the compass of taste. Here art—as only became clear later (too late)—was no longer cherished but fitted into a diagram as a collection of trophies. The Musée d'Orsay[5]—that temple of defilement—definitively closes the book of art history and opens the book of the art market. Not what is "good" but what has been "sold." The nihilism of taste[6] that was already formulated at the beginning of the century (in the Duchamp/surrealism version and the Bauhaus/constructivism version) has finally penetrated as far as the highest authorities. That nihilism "is" the contemporary taste; the unmasking of the taste debate, its reduction to other interests, that "is" art initiation today (abominable Bourdieu!). The entire nineteenth century has been Warholianized: art is a product like any other; art is the way one sells it.

Today, art is—not a problematic but rather a *mauvais objet*; I remember how art was presented to me precisely as the *bon objet*, the good object par excellence; good for identification, good for sublimation.

That value was immediately clear: art was respected. What contrast with today's nonrespect; neither for the work, nor for the visitor, nor for the intentions of art. In the presence of art you spoke little and certainly silently. Concentration was more important than loud reaction. The introverted person that art invited you to be, lived more intensely and—according to the unshakable belief—also better.

The break between life and art was crucial—at the concert you left the everyday behind, after the concert you took some of its unique qualities with you. Something that could resonate in a sigh, like an intensely cherished memory. You had the impression of having understood something, of having entered a territory of your mind that could have never been unlocked without that experience.

It was a crucial gift: the hypothesis of quality. That it was worth seeing the difference. That not everything was indifferently equal but that there was an endless palette of nuances. And that you could spend your whole life exploring and creating that palette. Become an aesthetic human being! That's what culture was for. Not a weapon to distinguish yourself but a possibility you could pass on. Art as the most generous proposition I ever received. There is nothing particularly exceptional or impossible about generosity. Museums are open, concerts can be attended by anyone, books can be consulted in all libraries. It is so obvious that you don't even register it as an achievement. Today nothing about this generosity is obvious anymore; on the contrary, it is distrusted, deconstructed.

Those who no longer see art as part of the art of living but as a way of producing, have very different priorities. They see art as intimately penetrated by a rhetoric of imago, by brand strategy. They consider a product something that must fulfill a somewhat obscure function; a product that must generate its own function.

Curators have become crucial stars, who deploy art rather than serving it. Through title and catalog, through combination and arrangement, the new type of curator organizes some thesis containing marketable social residue. It is always as urgent as it is noncommittal. In their hands art is a corps de ballet with which the impresario does what he wants. The curator as a director, art as a directed spectacle. The balance of power has shifted away from the artist toward demagogic curators.

Art as a product; a product without a function; an empty signifier that offers no resistance to not a single meaning. The ultimate incarnation of a commodity.

The logic moves toward an ever greater hermeticism, of shrewdness on the one hand and brutality on the other. What a hatred of the aesthetic hypothesis! What an iconoclasm is taking place all around me! What a forced vaccination against the organ of quality. An extermination campaign, declaring more and more no longer thinkable. Creating a wasteland for thinking. *Dépenser*; unthinking. This is our "cultural revolution."

Proposals that do not touch me but trap me. The fearful suspicion that the place where I could be touched is already gone. The fear that my problems are fake problems because all the others have evaporated, been anesthetized. The fear that I must make do with a cold artificial skin as if all the transplants and incisions have cut the nerve bundles and I only register external pressure. On the inside, I used to feel texture, warmth, chromaticism, rhythm, and contrasts. On the inside, I used to think mythology, see drama, interpret forces and read conflict. All that is left now is the fear of having only a blind skin. The fear of being blind. A skin as a radar screen with which I locate—determine distances and speeds—but am no longer able to receive anything from it inside. The fear of becoming a watcher at sidereal distance and no longer having any within-me at my disposal.

I often wonder what gives the visual arts such prominence in this process. Is it a matter of perspective, because I walk around museums more than I sit in the theater or read poetry, look at framed images more than I listen to music?

I often think it is not only to do with this unbalanced knowledge of mine. There is something about the visual arts that makes them the preeminent litmus for the test of this Zeitgeist. The *arts de l'espace* (Henri Van Lier) are of a very different nature than the arts that rely on performance. The body of the dancer, musician, or actor carries the artwork that appears. The limits of that body are the absolute limits of the work that appears. Every "performed" artwork finds its horizon in the possibilities and limitations of the body. All speculation is bound to that very concrete limit.

With the *arts de l'espace* it seems to be quite different. Architecture, sculpture, painting, and countless decorative arts are realized in permanent mediums, in matter that is not alive. They are not performances; they were made but do not know a performative mode. They arrive in the world fully complete. This completion connects them to what the living wants to transcend, and that is power. Power invests in architecture and in the other *arts de l'espace*, much more than in the performing arts.

Today, however, power no longer manifests itself in what is permanent (and therefore in what is ephemeral—for what is ephemeral can only truly take shape in what is permanent) but in feedback. Power no longer wants to be at the source of initiatives but in the place where the effects are measured. (One sees this transition most clearly in the contrast between the old paternalistic national broadcaster with its clear initiative and project and the new national broadcaster where initiative is ridiculed as headstrong pretension and where there is only room left for the execution of *feedbacked* assignments.)

So you see a perverse torsion in the sphere of the spatial arts. Power no longer invests in their symbolism. Pouring something into permanent matter has become ludicrous and conceptually unthinkable. Power no longer establishes, it experiments—with art, with opinion. The ambition of permanence has been lost to us in the most radical way. This also means that the perspective of impermanence is closed. After all, the actual is not the incarnation of the ephemeral but its radical destruction. In the actual there is only the now. Power disinvests in the spatial arts. The infrastructure of power has been replaced with the network.

We see how all spatial arts seek shelter under the wing of the performing arts. The spatial arts are always projections but today those projections do not wish to be fixed in a visual score but in turn be reprojected according to a performative logic. The stunning success of the projection-presentation, of the screen-idea, the introduction of sound (always a very strong injection of performative quality) all point in this direction. The spatial arts are organizing a massive escape toward performance. Only in this way can the spatial arts connect to the new face of power, namely as power over and power within the actual.

The visual arts shift away from (try to shift away from) their old position toward the performative, fleeting, and ephemeral. Visual artists as performers, visual work that wishes to be as fragile as a performance (great revelation and final rejection after seeing Beuys's *Honey Pump* once in a stairwell in Kassel[7]).

I expect the spatial arts to make my destiny become part of space, not to squander it in time. I expect the spatial arts to allow us to return to it—like to a house, a beloved city, an enchanting place, an acclaimed painting.

The balance between space and performance should be restored. Space is needed to think again that all power is thinking about the end of power, not about the boundlessness of power. To escape the hubris of experimental power, one must break the enchantment of the actual, and this requires the hypothesis of the permanent. The permanent drapes itself in space.

Notes

Contemporary Sophistry and the Poor Experience

1. The original Dutch text "Hedendaags sofisme en de arme ervaring" appeared in *De Witte Raaf* 62 (July 1996): 1–2. It was later included in Lauwaert's collection of essays *Artikels* (Brussels: Yves Gevaert, 1996), 207–219. Since 1986, the monthly magazine *De Witte Raaf* has inspired and furnished the conversation about visual art in the Netherlands and Flanders. The magazine publishes longer essays and reviews on visual art and its social, historical and political context. Starting in 1992, Lauwaert found a permanent home there: a total of eighty-three texts by him appeared in the magazine.

2. De Cauter, Lieven, *Archeologie van de kick: verhalen over moderniteit en ervaring* (Leuven: Van Halewijck, 1995).

3. Barthes, Roland, *Fragments d'un discours amoureux* (Paris: Seuil, 1977); *La chambre claire: Note sur la photographie* (Paris: Editions de l'Etoile / Gallimard, 1980).

4. Nacht, Marc, *A l'aise dans la barbarie* (Paris: Grasset, 1994).

5. Debray, Régis (1940–), French philosopher and writer. Debray coined the term *mediology* for the critical theory of the transmission of cultural meaning in human society. Lauwaert most likely refers to *Cours de médiologie générale* (Paris: Gallimard, 1991), *L'œil naïf* (Paris: Le Seuil, 1994) and *Manifestes medialogiques* (Paris: Gallimard, 1994). All these books are part of the Dirk Lauwaert Collection at the Library of Sint-Lukas Brussels (LUCA School of Arts).

6. De Haes, Leo (1949–), Belgian journalist and publisher. Author of the compilation of essays *Het doemdenken voorbij, over politiek en literatuur* (Dedalus, 1991).

7. *Andere Sinema* (*AS*) was a Belgian magazine on cinema, founded in Antwerp in 1978. It started out as a magazine accompanying the film club De Andere Film. Over time, it expanded its focus from cinema to image culture in general. Between 1988 and 1993, Dirk Lauwaert published fifty articles on film and photography in *AS*. During this time he further developed a format of compact reflections to a selection of images from photographic history which he introduced in *affect/afstand*, the catalogue to the 1987 Klapstuk dance festival. These similar contributions to *Andere Sinema* were later compiled and published as a limited edition box set *Belichte mensen* (Antwerpen: Andere Sinema, 1990).

8. De Vylder, Paul (1942–2022), Belgian artist, famous and infamous in the 1980s for the semiotic and iconological underpinnings of his striking installations and paintings.

9. "Don Juan and the Commendatore": Since the early seventeenth century, the Don Juan story has appeared in numerous variations (including Molière's theatre comedy *Dom Juan ou le Festin de Pierre* and Mozart's opera buffa *Don Giovanni*) which invariably harbor a certain sympathy for the dubious protagonist. Lauwaert here resolutely sides with the radical libertine who loses out to, or according to Lauwaert's reasoning in this text defects to the side of the reprimanding Commendatore. See note 5 to "Barthes, the Perfect Bourgeois" on page 199.

Reports from a Classroom

1. The original Dutch text "Berichten uit een klas" originally appeared in *De Witte Raaf* 50 (July–August 1994): 7. Since 1986, the monthly magazine *De Witte Raaf* has inspired and furnished the conversation about visual art in the Netherlands and Flanders. The magazine publishes longer essays and reviews on visual art and its social, historical and political context. Starting in 1992, Lauwaert found a permanent home there: a total of eighty-three texts by him appeared in the magazine. "Berichten uit een klas" was included in the collection *Artikels* (Brussels: Yves Gevaert Publisher, 1996).

2. Bergson and Foucault both taught well-attended classes at the Collège de France in Paris. Kraus was also a passionate teacher. From 1910 onward, his readings of his own and other authors' work became popular events in Vienna.

3. In "Doors Closed, the World in View: into the Classroom and the Cinema with Dirk Lauwaert" (*Sabzian*, February 24, 2021, https://sabzian.be/text/doors-closed-the-world-in-view), Herman Asselberghs probes possible overlaps between teaching and film-watching by way of "Berichten uit een klas" [Reports from a Classroom], "Objectieve melancholie" [Objective Melancholy], and other key essays by Lauwaert.

Critique of Enthusiasm. Culture, or the Event; The Accompanying Word: Passion

1. The original Dutch text "Kritiek der begeestering, over het manifest van het enthousiasme, de wetten van het klassieke, de zekerheden van de bewondering en de ontroering" appeared in *Etcetera* 26, no. 110 (2008): 6–11. It was later included in Lauwaert's essay collection *Onrust* (Aalst, Het Balanseer, 2011), 15–27. *Etcetera* is a Belgian performing arts magazine that was first published in 1983. At the turn of the century, the magazine focused on discourse formation, theory, and fundamental research. This text is the last of five essays (on theater photography, theater posters, and art criticism, among other things) that Lauwaert published in the magazine between 1989 and 2008.

2. In Greek mythology, Anchises was the father of Aeneas. His mother was the goddess Aphrodite.

3. Marthe de Meligny was the wife and principal model of the French painter Pierre Bonnard (1867–1947).

4. De Loore, Johan (1951–), Belgian painter.

Barthes, the Perfect Bourgeois

1. The original Dutch text "Barthes, de perfecte bourgeois" appeared in *Memo Barthes*, ed. Rokus Hofstede and Jürgen Pieters (Vantilt & Yang, 2004), 223–34. It was later included in Lauwaert's collection of essays *Onrust* (Aalst: Het Balanseer, 2011), 171–186.

2. Barthes, Roland (1915–1980), French semiologist, critic and essayist. For Lauwaert, Barthes requires no introducing or situating. He is without doubt one of Lauwaert's main inspirations and references, along with Serge Daney and Susan Sontag. Perhaps Lauwaert's abiding affinity with the French semiologist and essayist's trajectory can be traced back to the third Mostra Internazionale del Nuovo Cinema in Pesaro in 1967 where he, in the capacity of reporter for the magazine *Film & Televisie*, attends a roundtable discussion between Christian Metz, Umberto Eco, Pier Paolo Pasolini, and Roland Barthes, which starts off a new chapter in film theory. As a Belgian author, Lauwaert will contribute to this in his own way and territory. Bart Meuleman emphasizes that Lauwaert is in the company "of a compatriot he got to know at the festival: BRT producer Eric de Kuyper. Their experiencing that moment together is almost symbolic. Semiotics and structuralism will play a crucial role in the work of both in the following decades (as will psychoanalysis). Lauwaert and de Kuyper become bosom friends and will regularly cross paths throughout their lives." Bart Meuleman, "Hoe eenvoudig zou alles niet zijn, mocht ik een taak hebben… Dirk Lauwaert – de vroege jaren," *De Witte Raaf* 171 (September–October 2014): 10. Lauwaert is sure to have become acquainted with and carefully read Barthes's work even before the boost of this historic intellectual event: his *Mythologies* dates from 1957, his *Eléments de sémiologie* from 1965. Meuleman recalls that "in 1979 (following de Kuyper) he enrolls at the École pratique des hautes études in Paris to study semiotics with Barthes. But because the latter admits only a few students, he ends up (like de Kuyper) with Algirdas Greimas." Bart Meuleman, "Kroniek van een afgeladen leven, na de val uit het paradijs," *De Witte Raaf* 191 (January–February 2018): 8. Rudi Laermans points out that Lauwaert's intellectual practice is imbued with one of Roland Barthes's prime motifs: "Thinking contra the doxa that prevents autonomous thinking, writing contra the set of self-evidences that makes 'one' and not 'me' direct the discourse." Rudi Laermans, "Dirk Lauwaert als criticus. Fragmenten voor een intellectuele biografie," *De Witte Raaf* 192 (March–April 2018): 2. However strong the attraction, the differences are telling, according to Laermans: "According to Roland Barthes, thinking and writing revolve around finding the right balance between *saveur* [taste] and *savoir* [knowledge]. With Lauwaert, this tension implodes into a firm choice for the first term – for experience, which can neither be tamed nor systematized. Barthes situates his experiences within a theoretical register, drawing first on semiotics and then loosely leaning on Lacanian psychoanalysis. Lauwaert lacks these conceptual frameworks: his

criterion is a strictly personal being-affected which produces a myriad of affects and, while writing, makes his thinking tumble once more. Lauwaert is sometimes called 'the Flemish Barthes,' but he is not: a lot of taste, but little generalizable knowledge." Laermans, "Dirk Lauwaert als criticus," 5. That taste is also a kind of knowledge that can be learned, Meuleman experienced personally as a student in Lauwaert's class, where Barthes was a recurrent topic: "Via Barthes, Dirk Lauwaert taught us to *read*, to trace those strategies, and the promise that emanated from this was that we, too, would be able to dissect any phenomenon from our contemporary culture. A striking message: nothing is beneath our interest." Bart Meuleman, "Een feuilletonschrijver – de lessen van Dirk Lauwaert," *De Witte Raaf* 183 (September–October 2016): 11.

3. "the late Barthes about Japan": Barthes is fifty when he first visits Japan in 1966. After two visits he writes down his experiences in *L'empire des signes,* which appears in 1970 with Editions d'Art Albert Skira (Geneva) and will not appear in English until 1982 with Farrar, Straus and Giroux (New York). The designation "late" is somewhat misleading: Barthes will go on to publish nine more works during his lifetime, including some of the most important in his oeuvre.

4. Medusa is a figure from Greek mythology with a hairdo of writhing serpents and a deadly ability to petrify people who look at her. Depending on the reading, patriarchal or feminist, she symbolizes feminine horror and monstrous seduction or powerful survival and tremendous beauty.

5. At the beginning of the Don Juan story, the Commendatore dies in a sword duel with the womanizer who has just seduced his daughter. At the end, the statue erected in his memory comes to life to hold the libertine accountable and confront him with morality. See note 9 to "Contemporary Sophistry and the Poor Experience" on page 197.

6. Wahl, François (1925–2014), French editor of Lacan, Derrida and Barthes at Éditions du Seuil.

7. Monsieur Bouvet from *L'enterrement de Monsieur Bouvet [The burial of Mr. Bouvet]* by Georges Simenon (Paris: Presses de la Cité, 1950).

8. Jupien and M. de Charlus are two important characters from *A la recherche du temps perdu* by the French novelist Marcel Proust (Paris: Gallimard, 1917–27; rev. Paris, 1954; Eng. trans. as *Remembrance of Things Past*, London, 1922–31, rev. 1981; rev. as *In Search of Lost Time*, 1993).

9. "just as, according to Truffaut, one could not pat Hitchcock on the back either." Lauwaert refers to a passage in the interview book *Hitchcock,* in which the French filmmaker François Truffaut (1932–1984) biographically situates the detachment with which his British teacher looks at the world and thereby "almost always identified with the supporting role, with the man who is cuckolded and disappointed, the killer or the monster, the man rejected by others, the man who has no right to love, the man who looks on without being able to participate. (…) It is obvious that Hitchcock organized his life in such a way as to allow no one the familiar gesture of patting him on the back." François Truffaut, *Hitchcock* (London: Faber & Faber, 2017), 346–47. Originally published as François Truffaut, *Le cinéma selon Alfred Hitchcock* (Paris: Éditions Robert Laffont, 1966). First English translation published as *Truffaut Hitchcock* (New York: A Touchstone Book, 1967).

Portrait of a Role: the Intellectual

1. The original Dutch text "Portret van een rol: de intellectueel" appeared in *De Witte Raaf* 75 (September–October 1998): 7–9. It was later included in Lauwaert's collection of essays *Onrust* (Aalst: Het Balanseer, 2011), 67–95, with notes by the author (2–15). To these, the editors have added an introductory note (1).

   Since 1986, the monthly magazine *De Witte Raaf* has inspired and furnished the conversation about visual art in the Netherlands and Flanders. The magazine publishes longer essays and reviews on visual art and its social, historical, and political context. Starting in 1992, Lauwaert found a permanent home there: a total of eighty-three texts by him appeared in the magazine.

2. A naive intellectual is a tautology.

3. The op-ed pages of newspapers do not convey individual opinions but are a game of opinions.

4. Such as the Semaine de la Critique (in Cannes), the Prijs van de Kritiek [Prize for Criticism], a state prize for art criticism, etc.

5. The biblical "he who is without sin cast the first stone" is a perfect illustration: judgment is anchored in fundamental individualization, more specifically in guilt, the one thing no one can partake of.

6. Hence the misplaced realism that seeks to tarnish the exemplary and denounce it as mendacious manipulation. The exemplary does not want to be true but to function in society. Money isn't there to be exchanged for gold but to circulate.

7. Hence the logic of the tabloid press, the frenzy of the body. The abstract-exemplary must become radically concrete and tangible. The hyperrealism of relics.

8. The exemplary is a structure that puts the present into perspective.

9. I think of the baffling cynicism with which intellectuals responded to the social disasters of this country. No intellectual dimension was given to this just outrage.

10. Today, the reformers sit in director's chairs. It became a different kind of reform, though.

11. Roland Barthes's *Mythologies* is the historical high point of the ironic intellectual—we only get the contradiction in terms with hindsight.

12. See François Flahault, *La méchanceté* (Paris: Descartes & Cie, 1998).

13. Baudrillard is a prime example.

14. Ethel Portnoy once published a collection with the title *Vliegende vellen* [Flying Sheets]. Note by the editors: Portnoy, Ethel (1927–2004), Dutch poet; *Vliegende vellen: Schetsen en verhalen* (Amsterdam: Meulenhoff, 1983).

15. What irony, the dream of a scientific politics often heard around here!

The Sovereign Dandy

1. The original Dutch text "De soevereine dandy" was published in *Knack*, 2 July 1997. It was later included in Lauwaert's essay collection *Onrust* (Aalst: Het Balanseer, 2011), 146–156. *Knack* was founded in 1971 as the first Dutch-language news magazine in Belgium covering local news, politics, sports, business, and the arts. Between 1988 and 1998,

Dirk Lauwaert regularly contributed to the magazine. He wrote over two hundred book reviews and, from 1991, exhibition reviews.

The Rhythm of Thinking

1. The original Dutch text "Denken als ritmeren" appeared in *Andere Sinema* 110 (July–August 1992): 50. *Andere Sinema* (*AS*) was a Belgian magazine on cinema, founded in Antwerp in 1978. It started out as a magazine accompanying the film club De Andere Film. Over time, it expanded its focus from cinema to image culture in general. Between 1988 and 1993, Dirk Lauwaert published fifty articles on film and photography in *AS*.

2. Daney, Serge (1944–1992), French film critic and journalist. In 1964, Daney started writing for *Cahiers du Cinéma*. Between 1973 and 1981, he was coeditor of the magazine. He later started working for the French daily newspaper *Libération*, to which he had been contributing occasionally since its creation in 1973. This transition followed a shift in his writing on television. In 1991, shortly before his death, Daney was one of the principal founders of the film magazine *Trafic*. The collected writings of Daney in French were published as *La Maison cinéma et le monde* in four volumes (Paris: POL, 2001–2015), corresponding to three distinct eras, the *Cahiers* years (1962–1981), the *Libération* years (1981–1991) and the short *Trafic* period (1991–1992). The first volume was translated as *The Cinema House and the World, 1. The Cahiers du Cinéma Years 1962–1981* (South Pasadena, CA: Semiotext(e), 2022). See note 2, "The Classic Film Body", p. 202.

3. "Daney is an intellectual program…": Lauwaert links this program to three of his predecessors at *Cahiers du Cinéma*. Bazin, André (1918–1958), French film critic and film theorist. In 1951, Bazin cofounded *Cahiers du Cinéma*, which he would edit until his death. *Qu'est-ce que le cinéma?*, the collection of his influential writings, was published posthumously between 1958 and 1962 (Paris: Cerf) and translated as *What is Cinema?* (Berkeley, University of California Press, 1967–1974). Rivette, Jacques (1928–2016), French film critic and filmmaker. Rivette was editor-in-chief at *Cahiers du Cinéma* from 1963 to 1965. Bonitzer, Pascal (1946–), French film critic and journalist. Bonitzer wrote for *Cahiers du Cinéma* around the same time.

Mise-en-Scène: The Most Beautiful Word about Film

1. The original Dutch text "Mise-en-scène. Het mooiste woord over film" appeared in *Versus* 4 (1983): 58–63 with notes by the author (2,6,8,9,10). To these, the editors have added several notes of their own (1,3,4,5,7,11). Issue 4 of *Versus* documents the "auteur theory" era in film criticism and theory that started in the 1950s in the French film magazine *Cahiers du Cinéma*. Lauwaert's piece appeared alongside original Dutch-language contributions by Eric de Kuyper, Peter Delpeut, Mart Dominicus, and Jan Simons, among others, and translations of historical film reviews by the French critics Francois Truffaut, Jean-Luc Godard, Jacques Rivette, Eric Rohmer, and Claude Chabrol (who would go on to become famous filmmakers). The academic film journal *Versus, tijdschrift voor film en opvoeringskunsten* accompanied and helped define film studies as an academic discipline in the Netherlands and Flanders from the late 1970s until the 1990s. The journal was edited by the first Department of Film Studies in the Netherlands (Film- en Opvoeringskunsten, Catholic University Nijmegen) and published by the Socialistische uitgeverij Nijmegen, the academic publisher that made many important studies in the humanities accessible during the crucial years of change in the curriculum. Between 1983 and 1985, Dirk Lauwaert wrote five articles for *Versus*. "Mise-en-scène. Het mooiste woord over film" was included in Dirk Lauwaert's collection of essays *Dromen van een expeditie. Geschriften over film, 1971–2001* (Nijmegen: Uitgeverij Vantilt, 2006). The English translation "Mise-en-Scène: The Most Beautiful Word about Film" was first published by *Sabzian* on November 23, 2022: https://www.sabzian.be/text/mise-en-scene-the-most-beautiful-word-about-film.

2. Serge Daney, "Le délire critique," *Cahiers du Cinéma* 337 (June 1982): 84.

3. Daney, Serge (1944–1992), French film critic and journalist. Lauwaert refers to an observation by Daney in an interview with Andrew Sarris which was published in *Cahiers du Cinéma* 337, numéro spécial "Made in USA" (June 1982): 81–84. "Another thing that strikes me in the way films are approached here and in England is that everything is written with seriousness, with common sense but without passion. One feels that it would be wrong to rave about a film. This is quite peculiar—and slightly depressing—for a French critic" (84).

4. Bazin, André (1918–1958), French film critic and film theorist. In 1951, Bazin cofounded *Cahiers du Cinéma*, which he would edit until his death. *Qu'est-ce que le cinéma?* the collection of his influential writings, was published posthumously between 1958 and 1962 (Paris: Cerf) and translated as *What is Cinema?* (Berkeley, University of California Press, 1967–1974).

5. Godard, Jean-Luc, *Contempt*, 1963, FR-IT, 103 min.; Minelli, Vincente, *Two Weeks in Another Town*, 1962, US, 107 min.

6. "Mettre en scène c'est machiner, et d'une machination on dira qu'elle est bien ou mal montée." Jean-Luc Godard, "Montage mon Beau Souci," in *J.-L. Godard par J.-L. Godard* (Paris, 1978), 55.

7. Godard, Jean-Luc (1930–2022), French filmmaker and critic. "Montage, mon Beau Souci" was originally published in *Cahiers du Cinéma* 65 (1956): 30–31. This key text in cinema theory was translated as "Montage My Fine Care" in *Godard on Godard: Critical Writings by Jean-Luc Godard*, ed. Tom Milne and Jean Narboni (New York and London: Da Capo, 1972), 26–30.

8. Alexandre Astruc, "Qu'est ce que la mise en scène?," *Cahiers du Cinéma* 100 (October 1959); François Weyergans, "Qu'est-ce que le cinéma?," *Cahiers du Cinéma* 120 (June 1961); André Bazin, "Comment peut-on être Hitchcocko-Hawksien?," *Cahiers du Cinéma* 44 (February 1955).

9. "Ce qui est vu importe moins, non pas que la façon de voir, mais qu'une certaine façon d'avoir besoin de voir et de montrer." Astruc, "Qu'est ce que la mise en scène?," 16.

10. "L'idee d'une chose ne cesse de courir sous cette chose, sans qu'il soit nécessaire de renoncer à celle-ci" Weyergans, "Qu'est-ce que le cinéma?," 46.

11. Astruc, Alexandre (1923–2016), French filmmaker and critic. "Qu'est ce que la mise en scène?" was originally published in *Cahiers du Cinéma* 100 (October 1959): 13–16 and translated as "What is Mise-en-Scène?" *Film Culture* 22–23 (Summer 1961). The text is a reflection on cinema in response to Mizoguchi's 1953 film *Ugetsu monogatari*. Weyergans, François (1941–2019), Belgian filmmaker, film critic and novelist. "Qu'est-ce

que le cinéma?", a review of *Shin heike monogatari* by Kenji Mizoguchi, was published in *Cahiers du Cinéma* 120 (June 1961): 45–47. Bazin, André (1918–1958), French film critic and film theorist. "Comment peut-on être Hitchcocko-Hawksien?" was published in *Cahiers du Cinéma* 44 (February 1955): 17–18 and translated as "How could you possibly be Hitchcocko-Hawksian?" in *Howard Hawks: American Artist*, ed. Jim Hillier and Peter Wollen (London: BFI, 1996), 32–34.

The Classic Film Body

1.   The original Dutch text "Het klassieke filmlichaam" appeared in *Skrien*, anniversary issue, "25 years of Skrien" (September 1993): 6–7. It was later included in Lauwaert's collection of essays *Dromen van een expeditie: geschriften over film, 1971–2001* (Nijmegen: Vantilt, 2006), 213–216. The Dutch film magazine *Skrien* was founded in 1968 by students at the Film Academy, inspired by the French *Cahiers du Cinéma*. The original *Skrien* had a strong analytical, Marxist-leaning orientation, but the magazine gradually changed course towards a more accessible magazine about cinema, film, television, and new media. Lauwaert wrote seven pieces for *Skrien* between 1982 and 1998.

2.   "La Maison Cinéma" is a term ascribed to French film critic Serge Daney (1944–1992) (see note 2, p. 200. "The Rhythm of Thinking"). In France, already during his lifetime, Daney was regarded as a critic of the stature of André Bazin or Roland Barthes. His entry into English-language film culture was belated due to a shortage of systematic translation and perhaps (as one of his American interlocutors suggests) because of his tricky middle position between accessible journalism and erudite essayism. For that reason, it is no surprise that Lauwaert saw a kindred spirit in Daney. Both graphomaniacs subscribe to the chronicle as a means of deep and prolonged digging into the object of their passion. Their writings risk being too popular for academia and too academic for popular media. It is safe to say that Lauwaert, throughout his writing on film, implicitly and at times explicitly (as in this obituary) introduced the Daney spirit to Flemish readers who, from the seventies to the nineties, generally knew very little about French film culture. Lauwaert couldn't be bothered by that knowledge gap, as evidenced by his casual mentioning of Daney's key notion

"la maison cinéma." It was a notion no doubt close to Lauwaert's heart because it refers to the cinephile conviction that reflection on the image offers a way to understand both the world and one's own world. On the one hand, the "house of cinema" offers a dwelling for like-minded souls, establishes a community of friends, and serves as a home away from home for a self-chosen family. On the other hand, the "cinema house" provides a biographical foundation myth, a personal origin story allowing a life trajectory to be constructed or interpreted in hindsight. *Ciné-fils* Daney's autobiography was recorded near the end of his life in the form of a concluding conversation, published posthumously in the book *Persévérance. Entretien avec Serge Toubiana* (1993). Lauwaert left the cinema much earlier on his itinerary, making sure to report on his entry and exit in one of his seminal essays, *Dreaming of an Expedition*. (p. 141).

Seam and Pattern: Thinking Form

1.   The Dutch text "De naad en het patroon: denkende vormen" originally appeared as "De naad als denkende vorm," in *Patronen* (Ludion & MoMu, 2003) and in Lauwaert's essay collection *De geknipte stof: schrijven over mode* (Tielt: Lannoo, 2013), 7–20.

2.   *Burda*: First published as *Burda Modern* in 1950 by Aenne Burda and increasingly popular from 1952 onward, when it began to include patterns.

Dreaming of an Expedition

1.   The original Dutch text "Dromen van een expeditie" appeared in *Kunst & Cultuur* 28 (January 1995): 32–34. It was later included in Lauwaert's book *Artikels* (Brussels: Yves Gevaert, 1996), 197–206, and in his collection of essays *Dromen van een expeditie: geschriften over film, 1971–2001* (Nijmegen: Vantilt, 2006), 111–116. *Kunst & Cultuur* was the monthly magazine of the Palais des Beaux-Arts in Brussels. It existed from 1968 to 1999. Between 1970 and 1996, Lauwaert wrote more than two hundred articles for the magazine, on film, literature, and later photography.

2.   "a film about Spain: *Alcatraz*": possibly the Italian film *L'assedio dell'Alcazar*, a 1940 film about the siege of Fort Alcazar in Toledo during the Spanish Civil War.

3. "...that one film by Resnais...": Lauwaert refers to the impact of Alain Resnais's 1957 *Night and Fog* (FR, 32 min.) on an entire generation of cinephiles who did not hear about the recent war past from the mouths of their parents but had their eyes opened by the cinema screen. The formal interventions (text and image in counterpoint, literary sensitivity, mesmerizing travelling shots, ingenious montage) that Resnais introduced in this compact documentary essay and which he subsequently refined in his pioneering feature films (such as *Hiroshima Mon Amour* and *Last Year at Marienbad*), contributed to the élan of modern cinema. It was precisely the combination of a contemporary formal language and the elucidation of contemporary history that caused great upheaval, especially in his own country and in Germany. *Night and Fog* was not only a razor-sharp report about the horror of the Nazi camps but also mentioned the recent French collaboration and warned of the dormant survival of fascism on European soil. For film critic Serge Daney, the screening of the film at the *lycée* was a primeval scene of his profound relationship with film. In his memories of those years of encountering cinema (of the generation to which Lauwaert refers) he speaks about "those movies that watched us grow up and saw us—prematurely hostage to our coming biographies—already entangled in the snare of our history. For me *Psycho, La Dolce Vita, The Indian Tomb, Rio Bravo, Pickpocket, Anatomy of a Murder, The Taira Clan*, or *Night and Fog*, in particular, are unlike any other films. To the rather brutal question 'Does this watch you?' all of them answer yes." Serge Daney, "The Tracking Shot in *Kapo*," in *Postcards from the Cinema* (Oxford: Berg, 2007), 21. In the original text, Daney's question is "Est-ce que ça te regarde?", a pun on the French verb "regarder" which can mean both "watch" and "regard" or "concern", see: "Le travelling de Kapo", in: *Trafic* 4, Fall 1992, (Paris: Editions P.O.L.), 5–19.

Public/Publication/Publishing/Publicity

1. The original Dutch text "Publiek/publicatie/publiceren/publiciteit" appeared in *Obscuur* 9 (1997): 4–11. It was later included in Lauwaert's collection of essays *Lichtpapier: teksten over fotografie* (Antwerp: Fotomuseum Provincie Antwerpen, 2007), 128–137.

    The original version was subtitled "commentary on the publication of

photographs today in a couple of New Magazines: *AS/Andere Sinema, Obscuur, Images, Colours, Skrien,...*" *Obscuur* was founded in Belgium in 1994 to create a place for debate regarding "the place of photography in the visual arts and in social reality." It appeared three times a year until 2002. Between 1997 and 2002, Dirk Lauwaert wrote at least eight contributions for the magazine.

2. *Andere Sinema (AS), Images/Images*, and *Colours* were late-twentieth and early-twenty-first-century periodicals that proposed new ways of combining images and text. Dirk Lauwaert regularly published in *Andere Sinema (AS)*. (See note 1, *The Philosophy of Movement / The Rhythm of Thinking*, p. 200).

3. MTV, KETNET, and ARTE are TV channels catering to specific tastes and/or audiences: music (MTV), children (KETNET), art and film (ARTE).

4. "a Pied Piper of Hamelin": the medieval legend of The Pied Piper appeared in the writings of Johann Wolfgang von Goethe, the Brothers Grimm, and Robert Browning, among others. The phrase "pied piper" became a metaphor for a person who attracts a following through charisma or false promises.

The Blurred Photograph: An Old Debate

1. The original Dutch text "De onscherpe foto. Een oude discussie" appeared in *De Witte Raaf* 47 (January 1994): 18–19 and was later included in *Artikels* (Brussel: Yves Gevaert, 1996), 76–87. With regard to *De Witte Raaf*, see note 1 to "Contemporary Sophistry and the Poor Experience" (p. 197).

The Image That Yields Up Everything (Because It Has Seen Nothing)

1. The original Dutch text "Het beeld dat alles prijsgeeft (omdat het niets heeft gezien)" appeared in *Benjamin Journaal* 3 (1995). It was later included in Dirk Lauwaert's collection of essays *Lichtpapier: teksten over fotografie* (Antwerp: Fotomuseum Provincie Antwerpen, 2007), 141–151.

    Benjamin Journaal appeared five times between 1993 and 1997 and reports on the influence of the German-Jewish cultural philosopher Walter Benjamin (1892–1940). *Benjamin*

Journaal contained original essays by Dutch and foreign authors inspired by Benjamin's thinking.

2. "since 1931": Lauwaert can afford to get right to the point without any explanation. The article appears in a specialized journal for Benjaminians, so it is more important to indicate that he will not be talking about the author than to explain the year mentioned. As readers of *Benjamin Journaal* (are supposed to) know, 1931 is the publication date of "A Short History of Photography," the seminal essay by the German writer and philosopher Walter Benjamin (1892–1940) to which any theory of photography will have to relate. Lauwaert confesses his indebtedness to that Ur-text, and the same goes for authors Susan Sontag and Rosalind Krauss, whom he integrates into his argument further on in the text. Walter Benjamin, "A Short History of Photography," in *Selected Writings*, volume 2, part 2, *1931–1934*, ed. Michael W. Jennings, Howard Eiland, and Gary Smith (Cambridge, MA: The Belknap Press of Harvard University Press, 1999), 507–30, all citations on p. 510. "Kleine Geschichte der Photographie" originally appeared in *Die literarische Welt* (September–Oktober 1931).

3. "the version of Kraus and Livingston" and "the version of Sontag": Lauwaert refers, in telegram style, to two important twentieth-century approaches to surrealist photography. In the catalog *L'amour Fou: Photography and Surrealism* (Washington DC: Corcoran Gallery of Art, 1985), which accompanies their retrospective of the same name. Rosalind Krauss (1941–), American University Professor at Columbia University, art critic and art theorist, and Jane Livingston (1944–), American art curator, conclude that photography rather than painting or literature is at the heart of surrealist art. Lauwaert's quick labelling of their views as "style" is misleading: the ambition of Krauss and Livingston lies precisely in emphasizing and embracing the heterogeneity within surrealism and thus doing away with formalist categories of style in the (then) dominant art theory. Precisely in the photographic practices of the surrealists do they perceive unity in diversity. They refute the alleged incompatibility of the indexical, registering medium with the subjective dreamworlds of the surrealists by arguing that their photography does not by definition rely on trickery and collage but primarily on the preservation of traces of reality by means of darkroom techniques such as solarization,

rayographs, and *brûlage* or the deployment of pure registration with an eye to the alienating effects of depopulated locations or unusual frames and perspectives. A decade earlier, in *On Photography* (New York: Farrar, Strauss and Giroux, 1977), Susan Sontag (1933–2004), American essayist, novelist and filmmaker, uses surrealist photography as a springboard for a far-reaching reversal: the photographic conditions of surrealism (as Krauss titled one of her articles) lead her to the surrealist conditions of photography. In Sontag's view, the medium is fundamentally surreal because it provides the viewer with a duplicate of the world, a referential second-degree reality that appears in atomized fragments with no social or political dimension. Lauwaert's text essentially riffs on this core idea, whose logic of indexical duplication he fully endorses. Quoting from Lauwaert's discussion of the work of the French photographer and improper surrealist Eugène Atget (1857–1927), Steven Humblet places her at the heart of his philosophy of photography: "'Atget,' Lauwaert boldly posits, coincides with photography; he 'is so close to the 'essence' of photography, namely to be a device of registration [...].'" What Lauwaert appreciates in Atget's work is its dry, down-to-earth detachment. His surveying gaze is alien to any kind of subjectivity. Photography, the medium which according to the critic clings so tightly 'to the matter of things,' requires modesty, the willingness to place oneself at the service of the subject. Photography does not tell, but points out: photography is the art of showing." Steven Humblet, "'…een catastrofe, een revolutie; een omwenteling.' Dirk Lauwaert over fotografie," *De Witte Raaf* 191 (January–February 2018): 18. Quotes from Dirk Lauwaert, "Atget, fotograaf van Parijs," *De Nieuwe Gazet*, 18 december 1982.

4. "Barthes concealed that point. [...] Barthes underscores the temporal pathos of photography...": the hasty reference to *La chambre claire: Note sur la photographie* from 1980 assumes familiarity with the relationship Roland Barthes installs between *studium* and *punctum*. The studium points to the historical, sociological or cultural significance that makes the photograph legible and explicable. The punctum points to the subjective, emotional response related to the individual spectator and which escapes knowledge or comprehension. The elusive punctum happens to (or "pricks") the spectator and, according to Barthes, is peculiar to the indexical nature of (analog) photography. In the second half of his study

(which did not go unnoticed), he elaborates on the relationship between punctum and the photographic representation of time by means of a childhood photograph of his recently deceased mother. Barthes emphasizes the power of photographs to make us feel the passing of all things in the maelstrom of time: in his mother's photograph, he sees both her past projected and her past future foreshadowed. With his emphasis on the "indifference" and "a-emotionality" of the "automatic nature of the shot," Lauwaert counterbalances what he calls Barthes's "temporal pathos of photography."

5.   "the portrait of Dauthendey": Lauwaert refers to the famous passage in "A Short History of Photography" in which Benjamin draws attention to Karl Dauthenday's 1857 self-portrait with fiancée. In the gaze of the woman ("her gaze passes him by, absorbed in an ominous distance"), whom the photographer will find in their bedroom many years later, after the birth of their sixth child, with her wrists slashed, Benjamin discerns a dialectic between looking back at a past moment and anticipating a future event. As for Lauwaert's unspecified "breathtaking sentence structure," there are two options, either "Immerse yourself in such a picture long enough and you will realize to what extent opposites touch, here too: the most precise technology can give its products a magical value, such as a painted picture can never again have for us." or else "No matter how artful the photographer, no matter how carefully posed his subject, the beholder feels an irresistible urge to search such a picture for the tiny spark of contingency, of the here and now, with which reality has (so to speak) seared the subject, to find the inconspicuous spot where in the immediacy of that long-forgotten moment the future nests so eloquently that we, looking back, may rediscover it."

Moving House

1.   The original Dutch text "Verhuisd" appeared in *De Witte Raaf* 84 (March–April 2000): 4. It was later included in Lauwaert's essay collection *Onrust* (Aalst: Het Balanseer, 2011), 222–32.

Regarding *De Witte Raaf*, see note 1 to "Contemporary Sophistry and the Poor Experience" (p. 197).

2.   Koolhaas, Rem (1944–), Dutch architect, urbanist and essayist. Constructed between 1989 and 1992, the Kunsthal combines "3300 square meters of exhibition space, an auditorium and restaurant into one compact design." Its position, wedged between a busy highway and the network of museums and green spaces known as the museum park, allows it to function as a gateway to Rotterdam's most prized cultural amenities.

3.   "Centre Pompidou": Centre national d'art et de culture Georges-Pompidou, musée national d'art moderne: museum for modern and contemporary art in Paris; *Le temps, vite* was the title of the exhibition that ran from January 13 to April 17 in 2000.

4.   Lyotard, Jean-François (1925–1998), French philosopher; *Les immatériaux* was the title of an exhibition curated by Lyotard and Thierry Caput and presented at Centre Pompidou in Paris in 1985. The event-exhibition speculated on the rapidly changing experience of the contemporary world through technological tools and visitors' participation.

5.   Musée d'Orsay, Paris museum for Western art from 1848 to 1914, inaugurated in 1986. It houses the most important collection of impressionist and postimpressionist paintings in the world.

6.   "The nihilism of taste [...] (in the Duchamp/ surrealism version and the Bauhaus/ constructivism version) [...].": On Lauwaert's ambivalent relation to modernist art, see Dirk Pültau, "'Een kunst die nog dialogeert'. Dirk Lauwaert op de drempel van de abstracte kunst," *De Witte Raaf* 192 (March–April 2018).

7.   "Beuys's *Honey Pump*": Lauwaert refers to a large in-situ work by Joseph Beuys (1921– 1986), installed at Documenta 6 in 1977. Titled *Honigpumpe am Arbeitsplatz* [*Honey Pump in the Workplace*], the installation involved 150 kilograms of honey pumped through several rooms, as well as a rotating shaft of margarine. This use of unorthodox art materials was typical of Beuys. As was often the case, Beuys himself was also part of the exhibition, setting up talks and a discussion forum, addressing his expanded political concept of art.

Colophon

Lieven Gevaert Research Centre for Photography, Art and Visual Culture
Arts Faculty KU Leuven
Blijde-Inkomststraat 21 box 3313
B-3000 Leuven
Belgium

Author: Dirk Lauwaert
Editors: Herman Asselberghs, Robbrecht Desmet, Bart Meuleman, and Peter Jan Perquy
Translation: unless otherwise indicated all translations are by Sis Matthé and Trevor Perri
Layout and cover design: Theo van Beurden

© 2023 by Leuven University Press / Universitaire Pers Leuven / Presses Universitaires de Louvain.
Minderbroedersstraat 4, B3000 Leuven (Belgium).

ISBN 978 94 6270 385 8
eISBN 978 94 6166 530 0 (epdf)
eISBN 978 94 6166 531 7 (epub)
https://doi.org/10.11116/9789461665300
D/2023/1869/25
NUR: 652

Published with the support of LUCA School of Arts, LUCA breakout

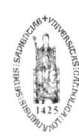 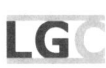 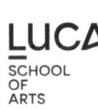 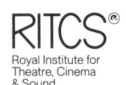 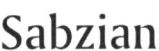

Cover image
Olympe Aguado. *Admiration !*, ca 1860, 20,4 cm × 15,2 cm, photograph on albumen paper, laminated on cardboard. Musée d'Art Moderne et Contemporain de Strasbourg, Collections photographiques Photo Musées de Strasbourg, N. Fussler. © Olympe Aguado